REDEPLOYED

PRESENTED TO:

_____

FROM:

_____

ON THIS ___ DAY OF _____, 20___

"Chad and Brian have written from their hearts about the challenges faced by our service members and their families. Their willingness to share their struggles and victories will encourage all who read this book. It takes a warrior who has been in the ring to relate to the challenges faced by our service members and families. These two warriors have hit the mark with this excellent book that should be read by ALL veterans!"
— **Lieutenant General Benjamin R. Mixon**
(U.S. Army, Retired)

"This book represents a practical, well-reasoned, and positive approach to life. For combat veterans it can bring focus and significance in the transition to a normal life with family and friends. I highly recommend this book for everyone."
— **Major General Bob "Hawk" Hollingsworth**
(USMC, Retired)

"The much anticipated co-authored book by two of America's heroic warriors is here. These amazing twin towers are shining examples of overcoming the odds that were so stacked against them that they put to shame all excuses to fail. Brian and Chad bring convergence of healing physically and emotionally to the most hurting in our nation."
— **Dave Roever (US Navy, Retired)**
Naval Special Warfare, Vietnam Veteran,
President of the Roever Foundation

"Hard hitting yet compassionate and poignant, Robichaux and Fleming don't sugar coat anything. The two address the cold stark reality head on: war is ugly, soldiers are trained to kill, and many struggle with the internal demons of what they've done and seen long after the uniform comes off. We all face a tough battle when coming home and trying to reintegrate into society is a fight that some servicemen and women unfortunately don't win. But armed with this road map the battles can be won and our country's most precious assets can be healed."

— Lieutenant Colonel Kelly Crigger
(US Army, Retired)
New York Times Best-Selling Author

"This is a book written BY combat veterans specifically FOR combat veterans. As a severely wounded warrior, it took some time to figure out, 'The mark of a man is not found in his past, but how he overcomes adversity and builds his future. Quitting is not an option.' This book fully captures this message and gives all those who struggle with the invisible wounds of war a path to overcome and reclaim their lives. If you have ever been to combat or are the loved one of a combat veteran who is still trying to rebuild their future, I highly recommend this book!"

— Lieutenant Jason Redman, US Navy SEAL (Retired)
Bronze Star (V) and Purple Heart Recipient,
Founder of WoundedWear.org

"The raw honesty of Brian and Chad will certainly resonate with their target audience: Combat Veterans. It will hit them between the eyes and hopefully help them see clearly, even if for the first time in a long time. The recommendations they both make are spot on and their examples are relevant and thought-provoking. A MUST READ for all combat veterans fighting the war within."

— **Dr. Tom Saunders, PhD (US Air Force, Retired)**
Professor of Psychology, Author of *Choices*

"This book explains that PTSD is a normal response to uncommonly stressful events. It is the mind's solution to protect itself so these events can be processed later. This book is a MUST-READ for any returning veteran."

— **Dr. Richard Wagner, M.D.**
Diplomate of the American College of Surgeons

"REDEPLOYED is a testament of the power of a faithful wife and gracious God in transforming a broken man. I love you Chad and I'm so proud of who you are in Christ".

—**Honorable Steve Toth**
Texas State Legislature

"In my life, I have met several brave and great men, each in his own field. However, I have met very FEW, who are brave, good, loyal and successful in more than one field. My brother Chad 'ROBO' is an exemplary family man, soldier, martial artist, professional fighter and altruist. Besides having fought for his country and on the ring in a relentless and effective way, he engages now on the most important and difficult task of his life: help the veterans to rebuild and save their lives. It is a difficult task, but knowing him, I am SURE lives and families will have happiness, health, and joy once again. Somebody has to step up and help the ones who gave their lives so we all could have freedom and peace. And I don't know anyone better or more qualified to do so than Chad Robichaux. The book is a great read, full of impressive facts and histories, and is a must read for all Americans to understand and appreciate what the real fighters do."

— Professor Vinicius "Draculino" Magalhaes
World Renowned Gracie Barra Jiu-Jitsu Trainer and Competitor

"In REDEPLOYED, Brian and Chad engage in a candid and cathartic discussion about hard fought emotional, psychological, and spiritual battles and the lessons they've learned. REDEPLOYED provides a refreshing blend of candor, faith, humanity, and humor to provide a road map and tools to help returning warriors and families navigate the realities of a post combat deployment. REDEPLOYED is a must read!"

— Lex McMahon, USMC Combat Veteran,
Son of the late Ed McMahon, Leading MMA Sports Agent,
President of Alchemist Management

"Great book! As a mom of a Special Forces medic who has returned to civilian life it gave me insight. Thanks for the work you do, may God shower His blessings on your work and the good your book will do!"

— Kathy Seei
Mother of US Army Special Forces Medic

"As a severely wounded combat veteran, I commend Brian and Chad's courage and leadership in addressing the silent wounds of war. From 'Mission First to People Always,' these brave warriors understand the true meaning of making sure no man or woman is left behind on the field of battle and, more importantly, on the home front. God bless them and God bless the United States of America!"

— **Major Ed Pulido (US Army, Retired)**
Combat –Wounded Veteran, OEF/OIF
Senior Vice President, Folds of Honor Foundation
Founder, Warriors for Freedom Foundation

"Chad and Brian have written a book that provides hope and potential healing to our nation's warriors! The overwhelming challenge of being redeployed from combat into 'normal' life is too much for our veterans to face alone. This book helps them to understand that they do not have to. With candor and transparency the tools are given that make living on purpose possible after combat. REDEPLOYED should be required reading for all combat veterans and the families who love them."

— **Jeremy Stalnecker (Captain, USMC Infantry) OIF**
Senior Pastor of Bay Area Baptist Church, Fremont, California

"Being the mother of a Special Operations soldier it has been difficult to see the changes in my son after his multiple deployments to both Iraq and Afghanistan. This book has opened my eyes as to why our soldiers are never the same. This book gives much needed information to the families of service members, as well as to the general public. Great job!"

— **Beverly Shoemaker**
Mother of a US Army Special Operations Soldier

"The book is very inspiring and informational. All veterans should read it, as well as their family and friends, or anyone who

wants to have a better understanding of the trials and tribulations soldiers face from deployment to the life that follows."
— **Nicholas Richter (US Army Infantry)**
10th Mountain Division, Combat-Wounded,
Afghanistan- Purple Heart Recipient

"Brian is a living testament to overcoming hardships and persevering with a positive mental attitude. He continually strives and has made it his life's mission to help veterans. This book is a great asset to service members and spouses that are coping with the stresses of life after the battlefield."
— **Eric Fleming (Corporal, USMC)**
Operation Iraqi Freedom Combat Veteran

"REDEPLOYED is a MUST read for the returning combat veteran, their spouses and immediate family. This book gives the veteran hope in knowing that he is not alone and is eye opening for anyone who knows someone or who has a loved one that is a returning warrior."
— **Corporal Jeremy Mahon, USMC,**
Iraq War Veteran- Squad Leader/ Scout,
1st Battalion 5th Marines
Professional MMA Fighter/ Muay Thai Fighter
UFC Trainer and 2-Time TXMMA Trainer of the Year

"REDEPLOYED should be mandatory reading for all returning combat veterans and their spouses. Brian and Chad not only remind you that there is a purpose to your life, they also layout a plan to help you find it."
— **Andrew Smith (US Army Infantry)**
Combat-Wounded, Iraq- Purple Heart Recipient

"REDEPLOYED is about overcoming the affects of war with practical strategies, humor, and real life courage. I am thankful to call both men mentors overcoming my own PTSD and hope this book helps others win the battle at home."
— **Billy Hertel (US Army Retired)**
OEF/OIF Combat Veteran

"Knowing Chad for many years and seeing his battle with PTSD and how he has overcome it helped inspire me to begin the fight that would change my life. With Chad's friendship and mentoring I have been able to begin to address my issues and become a better man and father for my family."
— **Jacob Kugler (US Army Infantry)**
Purple Heart Recipient

"This book, along with the Fight Club training at Eagle's Summit Ranch- Colorado, was a big help in letting me know that I'm not alone in my struggles with PTSD and TBI. I've come to realize there is a light at the end of the tunnel."
— **Frederick Spittler (USMC Infantry)**
Operation Iraqi Freedom

"Anyone looking for 'hope on a rope' needs to grab what's inside these pages. Brian and Chad are exceptional friends of mine and they will help lift you out of the obstacles you are facing. It would be a shame to have one more soul slip away to suicide. REDEPLOYED needs to be in the hands of every battlefield survivor!"
— **Scott Rimato FMP, Desert Storm Veteran,**
Founder of Patriot Ministry of Texas

"When your eyes have seen the images of war your soul knows pain that will forever be stored. But this book can give you a path, a marching order to a better way of life. If you are at the end of a journey or the beginning you have demons to fight, and there are no better ways for a warrior to attack a problem then through a military mind set. These men will go through the journey with you as you begin a new life, one without the same dead end trap that so many soldiers see when they come home from combat. Welcome to a better way to attack the war within. And thank you Chad and Brian for this incredible book that is more than needed."

— Daniel Walter (US Army), Operation Iraqi Freedom, Combat Trauma Peer Mentor

"A book that actually relates to everyday life after the war! It's easy to get lost in the reading and re-read over and over again. Great stuff, men!"

— Corporal Manuel Silva (USMC Infantry) Operation Iraqi Freedom

"Two heroes, two branches of service, one mission. These heroes are telling more than a story, sharing a common objective and inspiring a nation while at war!"

— Robert "BJ" Jackson (U.S. Army) Combat-Wounded in Iraq, Double Amputee and Founder of *The Right to Bear Stumps, LLC*

"Chad understands that for a warrior, sometimes the fight doesn't end when we leave the battlefield. With 18 warriors

giving up on the battlefield of life each day those are staggering losses. Chad's unvarnished talk and knowledge of PTSD has taught me that I couldn't keep fighting alone forever. He taught me that if I needed help then I needed to go and get it. Most importantly, as a warrior, he taught me to never stop fighting!"
—**Corporal Ramen Spears (USMC Infantry)**
Operation Iraqi Freedom

"As a combat veteran this book makes me realize I am not alone on my road to recovery and my battle with PTSD. Thank you for highlighting the symptoms of PTSD and for shedding light on this invisible injury. This book is a MUST READ!"
—**Sergeant Marty Gonzalez (USMC Infantry)**
Operation Iraqi Freedom,
Recipient of 3 Purple Hearts/ 2 Bronze Stars (V)

"Chad and Brian perfectly capture the struggles that combat veterans face when we return home to our families from a war zone. REDEPLOYED takes an in depth look at raw emotions and frightening experiences to which no combat veteran is a stranger, and how those emotions and experiences manifest on the home front. In many ways, I believe Chad and Brian are telling my story with this book, as well as the story of many other veterans. REDEPLOYED is a must read to understand how much our country owes to each and every one of its veterans!"
— **Sergeant First Class M. Travis Brantley,**
U.S. Army Infantry (Airborne)

"I am an Army veteran, a police officer, and most importantly a father to two sons. I choose carefully who I allow to influence my boys, and I entrusted Chad as one of those to teach my sons some lessons in life, and a little Brazilian Jiu-Jitsu. In personally knowing Chad, I can honestly say that God is using him as a vessel to help others rid their lives of those demons that haunt them. I recommend this book to anyone on that seemingly endless search for that peace and a happy life."

—Sergeant Michael B. Malone
Houston Police Dept.

"REDEPLOYED is one of the most powerful tools of hope and encouragement to our troops that are dealing with the struggles of returning home from war."

— Brad Hearon
President, H.E.L.P. INC
Burn Survivor, Motivational/ Youth Speaker

REDEPLOYED

HOW COMBAT VETERANS CAN FIGHT THE BATTLE WITHIN AND WIN THE WAR AT HOME

Publisher: Frisco House Publishing, LLC - Dallas, Texas

ISBN: 978-0-9889661-0-9
Library of Congress Control Number: 2013932207

Editor: Brenda Roever, Ingrid Carson

Cover Photo by Justin Trapp

Printed in the United States of America

Revised Edition 2017

REDEPLOYED

How Combat Veterans
Can Fight the Battle Within
and Win the War at Home

Brian Fleming
Chad M. Robichaux

FOREWORD BY
RANDY "THE NATURAL" COUTURE

5-Time UFC Champion and Hall of Famer

It was an honor for me to wear the BDU's of the 1980's in the US Army although there was not much more happening than a Cold War with the Soviets. I was proud to serve and ETS'd as a Sergeant, representing the Army and our nation as an alternate on the 1988 Olympic Wrestling Team.

Now more than 20 years later it humbles me to meet our service men and women coming back to this country, having represented us and our way of life with strength, honor, and conviction; many of whom have sacrificed so much! I appreciate all of you for your commitment and dedication to your families, your town, your state, and this amazing place we call home.

It is my sincere hope that you will take a hard look at this book and the insight and example set forth on these pages. They come from soldiers just like you, who've been where you've been and seen what you've seen. We hope you see the warm embrace that we welcome you back with and know that you're not alone. Keep fighting for your own sake now with all of us graciously at your side.

Thank you for all you've endured on our behalf. May you find health and God's peace in all you do now!

Sincerely,
Randy Couture

CONTENTS

ACKNOWLEDGMENTS

This book is dedicated to our returning brothers and sisters in arms. You are our heroes and we hope this book brings a spark of hope into any post-combat struggle you may face.

Sgt. Cody Legg, US Army
1/87 INF., 10th Mountain Division,
KIA June 4, 2008- Tikrit, Iraq

Brian Fleming

I dedicate this book in memory of my friend and roommate, Sgt. Cody Legg, 1/87 Infantry, 10th Mountain Division, KIA June 4, 2008 – near Tikrit, Iraq. You paid a price that most people are not willing to pay. When death stared you in the face, you didn't back down. Instead, you charged forward into the kill zone to save the lives of your men. I am honored and privileged to have known you and served with you. My only regret is that I was not able to be with you and fight alongside you that day. Your life and sacrifice will never be forgotten.

I'd like to thank my beautiful and faithful wife Jamie for sticking by me through the war, as well as through the many post-war battles we've fought together. You are one of a kind. I love you.

To my incredible, daring, and adventurous son… You've been a warrior since the day you were born. May you always fight the good fight and succeed greatly in all you do. You have what it takes!

To my precious daughter …You are stronger than you'll ever know and possess a love that can move mountains. You are a light in the darkness. You are beautiful. You are worth fighting for!

I would also like to thank the small handful of mentors who began appearing in my life immediately following my injury in Afghanistan. That I've come so far and been able to accomplish so much in spite of my war injury, I can only credit to your influences in my life. I am forever indebted to you for investing your time, life experience, and resources in me. You taught me how to live again and how to show others to do the same. It is on your shoulders I stand. Thank you.

Sgt. Foster Harrington,
3rd Force Reconnaissance Company
United States Marine Corps,
KIA Sept. 20, 2004 - Al Anbar Province, Iraq

Chad Robichaux

In memory of my friend Sgt. Foster Harrington, 3rd Force Reconnaissance Company, United States Marine Corps, KIA Sept. 20, 2004 - Al Anbar Province, Iraq, and to all of our fallen heroes. You paid the ultimate sacrifice for our freedoms. May you never be forgotten.

Thanks first to God, for allowing me this incredible experience and opportunity to live a warrior's life, and to continue my service in working for others.

To my beautiful wife Kathy who fought her own war in every deployment by giving up her husband. She has always been the rock of my family who dealt with the hardship and my fall when I came home. I am forever indebted to your love and grace to me.

To my three incredible children...You are my best friends and my greatest treasures in life. Thanks for giving me something worth fighting for when I wanted to give up. Of all the titles and accolades I've earned through hard work and sweat, the greatest title I'll ever possess is "Daddy."

Thanks to Dave Roever and Steve Toth for the invaluable life mentorship you have given me. Your gifts of friendship and leadership are invaluable... I swear to pay it forward to as many others as I can reach until my very last breath.

"Certainly there is no hunting like the hunting of man, and those who have hunted armed men long enough and liked it, never really care for anything else thereafter.

You will meet them doing various things with resolve, but their interest rarely holds because after the other thing, ordinary life is as flat as the taste of wine when the taste buds have been burned off your tongue."

— **Ernest Hemingway "On the Blue Water"**
(Hemingway, 1936)

Many of us have read this quote in the past. It is often spread across the back of military t-shirts and recited as a motivational tag line in training programs. To many of us, it was always just a cool saying—motivating. We thought we understood it, but had no clue. Hemingway knew something about the warrior who has been down range, who has wandered into the distant, foreign land in search of an enemy he does not know, but knows he must either destroy or be destroyed. He has clearly had an inside look at a warrior's struggle returning home and trying to reintegrate into a world where he felt he did not belong. *"You will meet them doing various things with resolve, but their interest rarely holds because after the other thing, ordinary life is as flat as the taste of wine when the taste buds have been burned off your tongue."* We couldn't begin to tell you how many combat veterans we've worked with who have been through a dozen jobs after being home only a year or two. Then there's the ninety percent divorce rate within five years of returning home from combat, and the fact that 75 percent of combat veterans will struggle with a drug or alcohol addiction within the first twenty-four months of returning home from war.

Reading Hemingway's quote, we now see it much differently than we did in our youth. It has gone from super motivating to super scary. We don't see an "OOH-RAH, HOO-AHH KILL, KILL" warrior in this story. We see a broken, hurting man. We see destroyed families and a sense of hopelessness, shame and abandonment. What can we learn? What can we do differently?

Every combat veteran eventually has to come to the realization that they will not redeploy to a combat zone. That's a tough pill for a warrior to swallow. However, if we were to redeploy we would be given an Op Order, a briefing. We would be told what known threats we might face, the enemy's current tactics and battle strategies. We would survey the terrain and geography of the battle ground that we would be fighting on, in order to set the mission up for success so that we would not only accomplish our mission, but come home safely to our families. We would be able to look at each known threat and either study SOP (Standard Operating Procedure) or devise our own plan within our teams as to how we would address these threats and defeat the enemy.

But when we come home from war, we are given no such briefings. We are not given an Op Order. We are thrown onto the battlefield at home unprepared for the coming battles many, if not most of us, will inevitably face. As with any unprepared group of individuals, the attrition rate is high. When we come home from war, whether a war in Afghanistan, Iraq, or any other war, we will REDEPLOY to fight again. It may not be a war abroad, but it is definitely a war within.

When we returned home from war, there were no known enemies or hazards for which we could prepare and plan strategies to overcome. We learned about these battles as they hit us head-on! Like many of you, both of us have had to fight an enemy at home we knew little about. We have just had to learn along the way—adapt and overcome. Fortunately, we've had a few good men help show each of us how to fight along the way and win.

Our hope and mission is that through this book each of our struggles, tough lessons, and valuable insights that we picked up along the way might serve as that OP ORDER for you, that threat briefing that you and any other warrior and spouse might need to discover a whole life together again as you reintegrate into civilian life.

This book is a map and it comes with several tools. It provides a lot of practical and proven ideas and solutions that are derived from each of our own real-life war and post-war experiences. Obviously, it does not have every answer to every question. Should you choose to use the tools and ideas in this book, it is likely that your life will change dramatically for the better. But nobody will do the grunt work for you. For better or worse, the outcome of your life is your responsibility. We cannot blame the government, the Taliban, or anyone else, especially since our military is an "all volunteer" force. Nobody put a gun to our heads and made us join the military and go to war, which actually speaks volumes about the caliber of person that makes up the American service member. The results you get in life are the product of your own efforts and are ultimately your own fault—whether good or bad. No excuses. Everybody has bad experiences. It's what you choose to do right now that will make the difference. Do it for yourself. Do it for your family. Do it for the other guy who fought alongside you in war and desperately needs help. You owe it to them, and you owe it to yourself.

CHAPTER 1

THE WAR WITHIN

BRIAN

During my fourteen months of recovery at Brooke Army Medical Center in San Antonio, Texas following the attack of the suicide bomber in Kandahar, Afghanistan I was required to go through a gauntlet of seemingly endless doctors' appointments. One day it was the neurologist trying to find a practical remedy for my daily headaches. The next day it would be a psychology appointment. Then the following day I would see the psychiatrist, just to make sure I had all the medications I needed (or wanted, really). Then I'd spend hours in physical therapy, learning how to use my hands again. I had third-degree burns and was unable to use my hands for several months following reconstructive surgery. But as bad as my physical injuries were—and they actually pale in comparison to those of some of my friends and fellow veterans who have been combat-wounded—I can honestly say that my "non-physical" injuries were far more influential (for better and for worse) than the physical ones.

Whenever conducting mentoring sessions with veterans and service members, as well as those civilians who are battling to get their lives back after enduring tragedy, I've often told them that I would rather be physically scarred and damaged on the outside than scarred and damaged on the inside. The outside of the human body is like the body of a car and the inside is like the steering wheel. If the outside of the vehicle is damaged and doesn't look too great, but the engine inside is clean and maintained, it will take you just about anywhere you want to go—no matter the distance required. However, if you've ever purchased a used car from a "less than reputable" neighborhood car dealership (yes, I've done it too), you know that even though a vehicle may appear appealing and well maintained, it is not always so. The next thing you know you are hiring a good lawyer to help you fight a legal battle to get your money back because though the vehicle you bought looked good on the outside, the inside was completely torn up.

Our physical bodies are a lot like the outside body of a car, but our inside (the mental, emotional, and psychological aspects of who we are) are like the steering wheel. We can look good on the outside, while at the same time be speeding down a road to complete destruction simply because our internal steering wheel is driving us down that road to destruction. I've watched it over and over again in the lives of people I meet. Whether this act is revealed through verbal or physical abuse, domestic violence, alcohol abuse, drug abuse (prescription or illegal), divorce, harmful addictions, it can be equally devastating. I've just about seen it all.

Sometimes you see a man or woman who seem to have everything in the world going for them—a beautiful family, plenty of money, successful and good at what he or she does. They have two cars, a motorcycle, the house with a white picket fence, and the statistical 2.5 kids—and this individual throws it all away. I've always been tempted to ask for their advice, "John, you had everything and chose to throw it all away. Can I buy you dinner? Teach me for a day how you screwed it all up." I'm obviously not seeking advice on how to fail in the way someone else did, but I will accept advice as to what brought that person to their downfall so that I might learn what not to do. A lot of great lessons can be learned from people who are failures. It's too bad nobody will pay them to speak at seminars. Their experiences can often prove to be quite valuable. I've been told by "gurus" in my industry that experience is the best teacher. But I've actually found that personal experience can be very painful, while other people's experience can be the best teacher. Many people learn what to do right by watching the example of another, but I've found it equally beneficial to learn what not to do from those I've been able to observe who have seriously screwed their lives up and thrown everything away.

To be successful in any area of life, you have to become a habitual learner. You have to commit to constantly educating yourself and always be learning something new. Whether it be through books, documentaries, live seminars, online courses, eBooks, or personal mentorship, you will never grow beyond your own willingness and level of commitment to learn more and become better.

CHAD

Unlike Brian—who modestly minimizes his physical injuries of being blown to hell and back by some lunatic with a warped sense of purpose—I personally did not get physically injured in Afghanistan. Well, not by the enemy, but that is a story I will save for another chapter. I, like so many of our combat veterans, suffered from the internal wounds, the ones that go unseen. In coming home from Afghanistan, I would face those demons head-on for the next three years of my life without the right help and healing. All I had was a few pills and a counselor who only seemed interested in hearing some war stories and watching the clock until he could end the session and cross his next number off the list.

Previously, Brian commented that he would rather be scarred on the outside than scarred on the inside. I have to agree. Well, some may think that's easy for me to say since I don't personally have the physical injuries. But I have actually said to myself: I'd rather have lost an arm or a leg than have lost my mind and soul. At many dark times, I have felt I was losing my mental stability. I felt I had traded everything good left inside of me for my service to my country and a terrorized people I had grown closer to and now had a desire to protect. With all that came a darkness, a hatred and a drive to win at all costs. I had to question my motives and my heart. Was I just serving my country or had I become a monster in the process? I know the answers now and I know that I am a whole man again. I did my duty. I love my country and am proud to have had the privilege to protect the innocent human lives at stake. But the road to that conclusion wasn't an easy one.

Now, on the other side of my own struggles and working with other veterans, I see clearly that I wasn't alone in this inner battle of self-judgment and worth. Many veterans come to me with the same thing on their mind that had been on my own. Not with the standard survivor's guilt, or the "poor me's" or "I'm so shaken up by all the killing." No, what I see in the real brokenhearted warrior is this:

- Why don't I feel bad about killing? Am I a monster? I expected to feel bad but didn't.

- Where was my empathy? Am I not even a human?

- How can I be a husband or father? I'm evil...

- Without a war, I have no purpose! If my family knew what I have done, they would think so badly of me.

These are such common thought processes of guys who have been in the trenches and put lead down range. The truth is, they don't feel bad because the military did their job in training these young men to do their jobs well. Let's not sugar-coat it, folks—what do the Army and the Marines train young infantrymen to do? Really? To kill! Period. End of trying to make it sound pleasant. A young infantryman has to be able to kill, and when he does, he can't just pack it up and go home. No, he has to wake up tomorrow and do it again. Why? Because war is ugly. Unfortunately, it results in death to someone, and the infantryman knows: It's better him than me or my buddy. It starts in day one of boot camp—the mental conditioning to prepare the warrior to pull that trigger, toss that grenade, or call in that fire support. To take another human life. If the training is done right, he won't hesitate, and he won't feel bad because he will feel pride over remorse, victory over defeat. And he will go out and do it again and again until he's home and safe. But when he's home and safe, he may reflect and he may think...why? Why didn't I feel badly? What is wrong with me? Am I a monster? That same training—and, let me make it known, that same very necessary training I agree MUST take place—the training that prepared him for war and sustained combat left him with an unanswered question. Am I a monster? Unfortunately folks, I don't think anything can be done differently. The training our warriors get is done for a reason, an ugly but necessary one...and the military does it right! I love our military and its training. However, war and its aftermath will leave young warriors asking this horrible question about themselves...and they will need help answering it. The well-trained warrior is not a monster. He is just doing what he is supposed to do. But for many warriors, coming to this conclusion will take a lot of time and some loving arms, as the satisfaction of surviving and killing seems so real and so the same.

Chapter 2

Some Things Are Worth Fighting For

CHAD

Why is it that when we watch a good warrior movie like *Braveheart* or *Gladiator,* we men feel like we want to kill something? Pick up a chair and throw it out a window, then eat a 72-ounce steak like a Neanderthal caveman? We have to understand who we are and what makes us tick. How can we even begin to fix our brokenness if we don't understand who we are, how we work, and why?

Anything that breaks requires the fixer, the mechanic, to understand these questions in order to trouble-shoot and start the repair process. It starts with identifying who we are and how we are designed. For me, I'm a man of deep faith, and I believe that God designed me to be a warrior and a leader. It only makes sense, since these are the only things I've ever loved or been good at doing. Knowing who I am gives me something to work back towards when I'm off tilt: a goal, and a hope. With that hope, I always find victory.

Some things that are the same can be created for different purposes. My wife, Kathy, and I, for example: We are both people, but as men and women we are very different. Just like motorcycles—you can have a Harley or a moped: both motorcycles, but very different. One is made to make you go fast, feel cool, and make noise. The other is made to be quiet and efficient. These two are much like my wife and I. I like to think I'm like that Harley—a little wild and dangerous but with a sense of purpose. While my wife is like the cute little moped sometimes she makes an annoying little winding sound, but she's cute, efficient, and so dependable!

In knowing that some things are created for different purposes, and so are we, it is important for us to not only identify who we are, but also strive to live it out. We have a Golden Retriever, Bowdie, who is seven years old. He was born and bred to hunt wild game and retrieve it. It's in his blood. When he was a puppy, we bought a big, fluffy down-feather comforter for our bed. My wife was so excited! I will never forget Bowdie's sinful little eyes looking up at us when we came home to find him in a pile of feathers and torn-up cloth. He was living out what he was created to be; shame on us for putting him in the house with that comforter. Now, seven years later, the fat couch-potato dog we have is far from his bird hunting blood line. If a duck flew toward the ground to its death and landed on old Bowdie's nose during one of his mid-day naps, I think he'd roll the other way and go right back to dreaming. Because of us, he's far from who and what he was born to be.

I love Bowdie, but I never want to follow his path. I want to be who God created me to be—a warrior and a leader. Maybe I won't be a warrior on the battlefield in my future, but I can still fight the fights worth fighting for my family, community, and for this country; and I can be a leader where others need me and I'm called to stand up and lead by the principles I believe in…and build my legacy under the things I stand for.

In the movie *Gladiator,* the new and evil Caesar addresses the gladiator slave to identify himself. He does this by turning and looking into Commudus' eyes:

"My name is Maximus Decimus Meridius, Commander of the Armies of the North, General of the Felix Legions, loyal servant to the true emperor, Marcus Aurelius. Father to a murdered son, husband to a murdered wife. And I will have my vengeance, in this life or the next."

Boom!!! Man, what does a man go through to learn his name with such passion and deliberateness? I can tell you that most people reading this book will have been through the same thing: a deep and lasting struggle. Pay attention to the words ahead and maybe you'll be able to identify yourself in such a powerful way.

When I meet other veterans who are at a life low, I always try to take them back to how proud they were when they graduated Basic Training. When I graduated Marine Corps' boot camp I felt like a super hero. I was on top of the world. Where do warriors lose that moment? When does it go away? When do we lose focus on our legacy?

You see, when you have these moments you have to fight to keep them. Your legacy, your honor, your integrity, and even your health are things for which you must fight. These are things that line up with our families and communities as things which are worth the battle. Yes, Some Things Are Worth Fighting For! This is the theme of our Mighty Oaks Program, Fight Club. Don't confuse this with Fight Club of the 1999 Ed Norton and Brad Pitt film, *Fight Club*—it's far from the same. However, Brad Pitt's character in the film, Tyler Durdan, makes a powerful statement that fits this point so well. He says, "How much can you possibly know about yourself, if you've never been in a fight?" So true! How do you know what you're made of until you've been tested? Do you stand alongside other men who have been tested?

I can remember being a young man, a teenager, and going through training to be a Recon Marine at the Basic Reconnaissance School (BRC) in Coronado, California. That is where Recon Marines and Navy SEALs go for their Basic Training. If you have never been to Coronado and felt the bone chilling cold of that water, well...you aren't missing out. The temperatures stay in the forties and I think God made it that way to make Recon Marines and Navy SEALs hard. I remember on a wet-suit appreciation day—which means no wet suits— laying in the surf zone with our arms locked and the breaks of the waves crashing on us. We were not even allowed push-ups or flutter kicks because it would warm us. With teeth chattering and every muscle tensed from the freezing water, I recall the instructors saying, "We are not leaving till five people quit." You are there with some tough and hard-headed Devil Dogs, but you are just praying that even your best bud will quit. At the time I thought it was so stupid, a rite of passage, an "I had this done to me, so I'll do it to them" thing…but that wasn't it at all. I know now that it was to show the ones who stayed what we were made of, and to know what a fellow Recon Marine was made of. That way, when you have to go into a cave or through a door in Afghanistan, you don't have to look over your shoulder to know if your men are behind you. You already know they are because you've seen them persevere in the worst; you've seen them break but keep going, broken. You know who you are, and you know who's on your left and right.

Ladies and gentlemen, everyone in life goes through hardship, but the difference the warrior has is what I just spoke… we have been through struggles and come out on the other side. That is what it is all about. Not what you go through, but how you come out on the other side. Through our battles we are forged into who we were born to be.

You know, the Bible repeatedly teaches this same lesson to us. Paul writes in Romans 5 that we are to boast in our sufferings, because we know that suffering produces perseverance; perseverance, character; and character, hope.

There is this story of a man who was walking through the forest and saw a caterpillar's cocoon hanging from a branch. The man thought it would be really neat to see the butterfly come to life and take flight, so he broke off the branch and brought it home. He hung the branch and cocoon over a jar on top of his windowsill and waited. One morning, he was walking by and saw the cocoon moving. "Today is going to be the day," he thought. So he took the cocoon and laid it on the table. Then he grabbed a cup of coffee and pulled up a chair and began to watch and wait for the big show. All of a sudden, it started to happen. The cocoon started shaking violently and in a moment there was a small crack on the surface. The man grew more and more impatient as the butterfly's little feet struggled to pull the crack in the cocoon's skin open. The head popped out but it just didn't seem as if the butterfly would make it out on its own. In frustration the man picked up the cocoon and carefully tore it open. Out came this beautiful big butterfly! However, as the butterfly spread its wings, it fell flat on the table and died.

It was the struggle! It was the struggle that was necessary for the butterfly to be what it was meant to be; it needed the struggle to spread its wings and fly. You see, God designed it that way. As the butterfly pushes its wings against the cocoon walls, it releases a chemical needed to strengthen the wings. The struggle is part of the process, part of the design. Robbed of the struggle, the butterfly could not live. It never became who it was born to be. Persevere through your struggles; there is value in it…but you have to wait till you're on the other side to see it, and see what its purpose is in molding you to be who you were born to be.

I joined the United States Marines Corps in 1993 and entered into Special Operations as a Force Recon Marine. It would not be until ten years later that I would see war. I was deployed for eight tours of duty in the Afghanistan War on Terror. After four long years of deployments, I spent years recovering from Post-Traumatic Stress Disorder.

PTSD rattled my faith and eroded my relationship with my family and friends. At times I felt like my body was just going to shut down. I had been physically hurt many times in my life, but this was different: this was hopeless. It was terror. There were other times I felt like there was a monster inside of me, and I would hide from everyone I loved. My paper-thin version of my faith as a Christian could not hold up. I was broken, with no foundation or safe place to fall; in a downward spiral, feeling that my demise was imminent somehow. It may sound crazy, but to me it was so real. I had a paralyzing fear that I was going to be committed; if anyone knew how I really felt inside they would put me in a straitjacket and lock me up in a hospital. Because of this, I felt alone and isolated, so I kept many of my fears and thoughts to myself for a very long time.

The counselor who was seeing me searched to discover something productive to reintegrate me into a normal life. He asked me what I enjoyed besides the military and I told him about my passion for martial arts. Separate from my military career, I was a lifelong martial artist. At this time, I was already 6-0 as a professional Mixed Martial Arts (MMA) fighter. Starting at just five years old, I had earned black belts in Karate, Japanese Jiu-Jitsu, American Jiu-Jitsu, and Gracie Brazilian Jiu-Jitsu. I am a black belt under the legendary Master Carlos Gracie Jr. I was promoted to black belt in Brazil, where my friend and World Champion David

Vieriera tied my belt on in the favelas in the streets of Rio De Janiero. I loved training with the inner city grapplers of Rio's favelas; it was like playing basketball in the parks of Harlem— where the real players play—so it was such an honor to earn my black belt there. I went on to earn a second degree black belt under one of Master Carlos' top Professors, Vinicius Magalhaes, "Draculino," a great man and friend on and off the mats. Jiu-Jitsu has always been a huge part of my life, and in my worst times it has been a grounding place for me. I had competed on a world-class international stage, and I would eventually earn a record of 17-2 as a Professional Mixed Martial Arts Fighter. At one point I was ranked #1 in the USA and #6 in the world in my weight class, competing in Showtime's StrikeForce, the main event of Bellator FC on MTV2, and won a World Title Belt for HD Net / AXS TV's Legacy FC.

The success as a fighter gave me temporary relief from my PTSD. On the surface, it looked like I had overcome my Afghanistan demons. I would use my platform on television to encourage civilian support of other mentally and physically wounded veterans, but inside I had never healed. Three years after coming home my family faced divorce and we separated. It was tragic and I was reliving the mistakes of my father who came home from the Marine Corps as a broken Vietnam Veteran and ruined our family during my childhood. How naive was I not to see it coming? How arrogant was I? I had destroyed my family out of my pride to refuse help, and my ignorance to turn my back to a wife who was trying to love and help me. In isolating myself from her and from everyone close to me I found myself alone. I built a wall I thought would keep everyone close to me out. Brick by brick I isolated myself to protect everyone from knowing who I had become, but what I didn't realize was I had not only built a wall to keep them out... I had built the walls of a prison cell that kept me in, thereby condemning myself to it with every bit of darkness I had allowed into my life. I was lonely, angry, and bitter. It was only a matter of time before I did something stupid, and I did by turning to women for comfort and attention. I never thought I would stoop so low and allow infidelity to take root in my life, but it did and there I was at rock bottom and wondering how I let myself get there. It wasn't what I wanted and I wasn't where I wanted to be, but it was the work of my own hands that put me there and for the first time in my life felt as if I had lost all direction. I had been a traitor to my family, kept them out, and gave up hope on a future together.

One day, my wife said to me, "Chad, how can you go to war and fight for our country and be willing to die for your buddies, how can you can train so hard and show so much discipline to train for combat or to fight for a championship in the cage, BUT when it comes to your family you just quit?" Ouch!!! First of all, she could not have been more right. And secondly, I had never been called a quitter, and it stung!

I hit my knees in a lonely apartment and cried. I decided to put the challenge my wife laid before me into action and actually fight for the things that mattered most: my family and my healing.

Later, my faith would be restored. I prayed for God to restore my feelings, take away the coldness and bitterness that had consumed my heart, and give me empathy and compassion once again. AND HE DID! I wept like a child for hours. All those years of pain, hate, and anger surfaced in a moment. Then I found the will and ability to respond to the challenge of my wife's words. I committed to apply the same character, work ethic, discipline and loyalty that I had displayed as a Force Recon Marine and as a World Class Athlete into the areas of my life that mattered most. It was a complete shift of priorities. I would now fight for my faith, my character, my integrity, and my family. I would have the same never-quit attitude I had displayed throughout my entire professional life—only now, where it counted most.

Shortly after stepping onto this new path, I was approached by Tierce Green, a men's pastor at a church I had attended. He was interested in starting a project connecting the discipline of a fighter with the discipline of an authentic man of God. He asked if he could use my training center as a theme and backdrop to film the series. When you look back, you can always see God's hand in putting things together. I think Tierce was equally amazed when I told him my story and we agreed to integrate it into the curriculum. The series was called Fight Club, and it was a huge success. In fact, I went through it myself, and personally going through the final product of Fight Club gave me the tools and the foundation to rebuild my faith that I needed to complete the challenge I had taken on in my own life. This was the solid foundation I was lacking, the template for true manhood, and although it wasn't an easy road, it was a road with clear directions for where I was headed and the tools I would need to get there.

Today, my family and I share a story from tragedy to triumph about the struggles our warriors face in returning home. We have dedicated our lives to share this victory and to mentor others like us. We travel and speak around the country to educate others about America's role in helping warriors who are returning home—many who are wounded deep below the surface and now need to learn how to fight a different kind of enemy.

I was privileged to serve under the leadership of Dave Roever, and am now the founder of the Mighty Oaks Foundation, where Kathy and I administer programs dedicated to helping our combat heroes and their families who are suffering from the unseen wounds of combat stress and PTSD. Our most successful tools to date have been our Legacy Programs and our Spiritual Resiliency Programs, that help both our combat heroes find their way home and those that are deploying have a strong foundation.

As a Professional MMA fighter, I've had the privilege of training with some of the world's very best athletes and coaches. In my last two training camps I've had the huge honor to work with Randy Couture, and one of his long-time wrestling partners Brad Anderson, Olympic Wrestling Team Alternate. These two men are such a definition of men of grit and warrior's spirit. Most everyone knows Randy as The Natural, UFC Champion, Hall of Famer, and one of the sport's cornerstones, or for his roles in many great action films such as *The Expendables, I & II.* What many don't know is Randy's kindness, character, down-to-earth attitude, and natural ability to pass these traits onto others through his coaching.

One day when training with Randy, he talked about "visualizing the win." I have heard this all my life in martial arts. However, Randy had a passion about it and I knew he had something valuable to share, so I took it all in. After one of Brad's grueling torture/ training sessions for my fight against UFC Veteran Joseph Sandoval, Randy ran me through a visualization training session. As I lay on the mats, drenched in sweat and still catching my breath from two hours of work, Randy's voice took me into the future to the night of the fight. He took my mind on a visual journey, starting in my locker room warming up to the minutes out from the event coordinator. I walked out to the music I had selected for my entry to the cage, Johnny Cash's *"Ain't No Grave."*

Randy's voice continued, "The crowd is cheering your name, everyone's watching." I can remember every detail, down to the Vaseline being wiped onto my eyebrows and the bridge of my nose. As my mouth piece was placed in my mouth, it was time. I was walking into the cage and the door was shut. It was me and Sandoval alone, with only a referee to guide the action that would soon take place between us. When the referee said, "Fight," I circled left to the southpaw's right side like I had trained hundreds of times. It was so real: all the details we had worked in training, my strengths and Sandoval's weaknesses were visualized. In a moment I had walked through my opponent. Randy's voice took me even through the moment where my hands were raised in victory.

One month later, there I stood, face to face with Sandoval. The visualization was real life now, yet it would all play out exactly how we had spoken it, seen it, and claimed it—even through the moment where my hands were raised in victory. It was an amazing night in my career as a fighter, but as a man who has faced struggles and as a mentor to others who have faced the hardships of life, Randy taught me a valuable lesson. Have passion in your future, visualize your victories, and claim them— all the way through the moment when your hands are raised in victory.

BRIAN

Chad makes some great points in this chapter about fighting for the things in life that matter most. In working with military service members and veterans over the years, this is something I have seen countless times: So many men and women are willing to fight and die for their buddies in war, yet so often they come home and allow their families—the most important thing in life—to fall apart. This is ultimately one of the goals of our nation's enemies: to see our way of life destroyed.

Some things in life are worth fighting for; realizing the *right things* to fight for can be half the battle.

CHAPTER 3

"BROKE" OR "HURT?"

CHAD

I recall my first years in the Marine Corps, when I was much younger, and far more durable.

I was only seventeen years old when I enlisted in 1993, and in just over a year I had started on the path to accomplish one of my biggest childhood dreams: to be a Force Recon Marine. I took the "Recon Indoc" in California, where a hand-selected group of the very best Marines get to try out for a chance to earn the (0321) Recon Man MOS (military occupational specialty). The average Recon Indoc will have a group of about fifty stud Marines who were hand-selected to try out, and only a handful will get picked up…and this is just to start the path to becoming a Recon Marine.

I always hear everyone complain about how difficult it was, but I remember being so pumped I probably smiled ear to ear from beginning to end. It starts off with a standard Marine Corps physical fitness test (PFT), and you're expected to get maximum results on the three-mile run in eighteen minutes, twenty pull-ups, and eighty sit-ups. My run time was under seventeen minutes and I was nowhere near the front of the pack. However, my strongest attribute was the pool and it was up next. We ran from the PFT to the "swim tank," put on a pair of cammies (the Marine Corps term for the camouflage uniform), and straight into the pool for a thirty-minute water tread, which ended with a 500-meter timed swim. Then we had to do a series of drills in the water under a name I became all too familiar with in the coming years:"water aerobics," followed by sprints and drills to push your endurance. I think the last of the events was a twenty-five meter swim holding a ten pound brick out of the water. After that, we went to the standard Marine Corps obstacle course and completed it twice, timed, back-to-back, and ending each time with a rope climb. We wrapped up the day's work out with a five-mile ruck run accompanied by a fifty pound sandbag in our packs and a rubber M-16 in our hands. The day wasn't over, as we had a fast turnaround to get looking our Marine Corps best and present ourselves before an interview board…standing tall and looking sharp. After all that, you think you'd become a Recon Marine on the spot. Far from it. The months ahead are filled with academics, physical training, and skill-building. It is a long road to one of the best jobs in the world.

One of the things I always say when I speak alongside Dave Roever is: we all get hurt. Some people lose their legs, some their minds. Some of us get hurt in war and some of us in life at home. The bottom line is: everybody faces struggles. It's part of life and our growth. But it's not what we go through—it's how we come out on the other side of it that counts. When the dust settles, will you be lying on your backside or standing tall?

I always discuss my experience with PTSD and my reintegration into life as a civilian and the struggles my family and I experienced. What I never mention is my physical injuries. I've talked about them, but rarely do I even mention them in a group setting. In working on this book, I began to question why. I have four broken vertebrates from two separate incidents, and on one of the vertebrate, all three of the transverse and spinous processes are broken off.

The first time I "broke" my back—errr, I don't like the word "broke" and I'll explain why in a bit—but the first time was in 1994. I was on a Joint Task Force-6 (JFT) Counternarcotic Mission. I did a lot of these in my first four years in the Marine Corps. It's a type of mission where the Marine Corps supports the Department of Defense to suppress the flow of narcotics and terrorism into the borders of the United States. During a time when there were no wars to deploy to, this was a great experience for a young Marine pumped up to serve his country and put his training to use.

This particular mission was not directly on the border but in the Cleveland National Forest of Southern California, where there were suspected narcotics caches and underground grows for marijuana. I was the point man on a six man patrol. I can't recall the exact date but, man; I can remember the heat, so it was no doubt the peak of summer. Not only was it hot because it was Southern California, but the brush was so thick and the poison oak vines were so unavoidable that you had to crawl and tear your way through them in many places. If you've never been in a brush infested valley in the cold, then you can't understand how the humidity from the vegetation lowers the temperature by ten degrees combined by the dampness. Just the same, the valleys we were working in for this thirty-day operation were ten degrees hotter and married with a 100 percent increase in humidity. It was a nasty environment.

The combination of the heat and the thick vegetation were not conducive to tactical movement, so all movement had to take place at night. The easiest routes were the stream beds. One night, while on point, I made a nearly fatal error. With my inexperience and lack of ambient light, I was struggling with the depth perception of my NODs (night observation device), AN PVS-7s, so I took them off to try to go on my night vision. As I was leading the patrol through the stream bed, struggling to see, I could hear the water flow of the stream increase. What I didn't know, my next step would reveal to me—a waterfall. As I stepped over the edge I was immediately turned upside down by the weight of my heavy ruck sack. I didn't have my waist strap buckled on my ruck so it pulled me by my shoulders and exposed my lower back. After falling about fifteen feet in the dark, I landed on the stream floor below, which was a bed of Southern California's finest collection of large boulders; my lower back found a big one. I had the wind knocked out of me and it seemed forever before my teammates made their way down the banks and through the vegetation to get to me. After getting my breath I couldn't move my legs. I remember being really embarrassed for making such a goofball mistake and taking everyone off of mission. I would later learn that Recon Marines and big rucks sacks fall, often! But, at that time, my pride was hurt and my legs weren't working.

After about an hour of trying to establish communications, my team was able to call in for Medical Evacuation (MEDEVAC). Fortunately, within that hour I was able to start moving my legs and, with help, even get to my feet. After a prescription of Naprosyn, muscle relaxers, and a back brace, I just needed six weeks of rest to be fit for duty again. I was young and durable and I was not going to lay up, broken.

The second incident where I injured my back was another inglorious moment of "idiocracy"—only this time not on my part. Why couldn't my story be just a little cooler than people doing stupid stuff and me getting hurt? Well, my partner and I were relieving two teammates in a place I frequented all too often in Southeast Asia. We were riding in the open bed of a Hi-Lux Toyota pickup truck...yes, the official truck of the Taliban. The guy driving— and to protect his identity, let's just call him Mr. Butthead—was being a butthead and driving down this high mountain road like Danny Beauchamp, World Champion Off-Road Racer, when he suddenly hit—yes, another boulder. What is it with me and boulders? Did I throw too many rocks in the pond as a kid and this is payback? I was sitting flat on my butt and launched about fifty feet in the air!

Okay, that is the story I told my kids, and they believed it. Honestly, I don't know how high I went up; I just know that I landed flat on my butt and felt a crunch in my lower back and a compression all the way up to my neck. It hurt and I was ticked. We were on a long road with no exits for over ten hours, so my partner and I decided to do what good Americans overseas do: commandeer a ride with the strangers in the vehicle behind us. They were obliged. Mr. Butthead thought we were joking, but we stuck to our bitterness and refused to ride with him. We were enjoying the company of our new friends. There would be no MEDEVAC this time, and I'd spend the next two months sucking it up before ever going back to a doctor to check it out. At this time in my life I wouldn't say I was young and durable anymore, but I still was not going to lay up, broken.

You see, I never accepted that I "broke" my back twice. I only allowed myself to believe that I "hurt" my back twice. I guess in my subconscious it was easier to drive forward believing I was hurt and not broken. Years later, I dislocated my femur head from my hip socket while doing Brazilian Jiu-Jitsu training. I was carried off to the doctor and when he came out with the x-ray, I remember his surprise. He said, "When was the last time you broke your back?" I responded, "I never broke my back, I hurt it a few times." Hard-headed! The point is this: even after years of knowing I had jacked up my back badly, after refusing surgery and giving myself rehab through years of core strengthening, I still wouldn't admit I had a broken back. I still struggle today with it. The word "broken" is just too permanent, but the word "hurt" has hope for healing.

No matter what happens in our lives—whether we see ourselves as "hurt" or "broken"—why not be optimistic and choose to think that something great could come out of a bad situation? We all know how powerful retrospect can be; we can all learn and be so inspired by the stories of others facing tragedy, and finding victory in the end. If this is the case for others, then why not trust that process in our own lives? As a man of faith, I believe that sometimes the greatest testimonies in life happen when the devil tries to do something to destroy us and God turns around and uses that very thing for good.

Of all the stories I have heard about victory over life's tragedies, I think one of the most inspiring is Helio Gracie's story. I'm sure this is partly because I am passionate about the art of Brazilian Jiu-Jitsu and I have such a close lineage to this story, but it's also because I love what Helio's life was about, what he stood for as a man, and what kind of legacy he left behind. Helio's life demonstrated the kind of perseverance to achieve greatness that is rarely witnessed in a lifetime. I always enjoy telling this story to new students embarking on the journey of Brazilian Jiu-Jitsu (BJJ), which is inarguably the most dominant martial art in the world today because of one sickly little boy.

In 1914, a man named Mitsuyu Maeda arrived in Brazil. Maeda, also known as Conde Koma (which translates as the Count of Combat), was a student of Jigoro Kano, one of the very last true Samurai trainers in Japan. Maeda was said to be his best student. After traveling the globe, competing undisputed as a martial artist and propagating the art of Judo and Traditional Japanese Jiu-Jitsu to the world, Maeda decided to help build a Japanese Colony in Belem do Para, Brazil. I don't know a whole lot about Maeda's personal life, but I would have to say I liked him. For one thing, he loved Jiu- Jitsu; and, secondly, he was only five feet, four inches tall—a man with whom I could see eye to eye.

At that time, the Gracie family had no involvement in martial arts. Gastao Gracie was the father of eight children, five of whom would become the pioneers of Brazilian Jiu-Jitsu. He was in the diamond business and did some trade with Maeda. Gastao asked Maeda to train his oldest son, Carlos Gracie, who was fourteen at the time. Carlos was said to be a bit of a rambunctious teenager, so it made sense for him to be schooled in a Japanese tradition of discipline and self-defense. Maeda taught Carlos for only a few years, but Carlos continued to train with his brothers Osvaldo, Gastoa, and Jorge in the Japanese style. The brothers opened the Gracie Jiu- Jitsu School in Rio De Janiero in 1925.

At that time, Helio Gracie was fairly young and didn't train with his older brothers. Another thing that kept Helio back was that he was a very frail and sickly child; he would have fainting spells, and struggled to even climb a flight of stairs. However, Helio had a fighter's heart and a genius mind. He watched his brothers train and teach, and in his mind he developed a modified version of Jiu-Jitsu, on that utilized more leverage and technique to compensate for his frail and weak body. Those techniques would be discovered when Helio was sixteen years old. Carlos had a private class scheduled for an older man who was the Director of the Bank of Brazil, Mario Brandt, but Carlos was late. Helio rose to the occasion and offered to teach the class. The man loved Helio's teaching so much that he requested he continue all future classes with him, and a Jiu-Jitsu legend was born.

Word spread of Helio's teaching ability and techniques, and his students' skills soon surpassed those of his brothers. It didn't take long for Carlos and the other brothers to realize that Helio was on to something, and they all joined in. It was then that Gracie Brazilian Jiu-Jitsu was born. Helio not only continued as an instructor until his passing at the age of ninety-seven, but also fought professionally in no-weight-limit fights nineteen times. He was recognized as Brazil's very first sports hero.

Today, Brazilian Jiu-Jitsu is no doubt the most effective and dominant martial art practiced. It is the only art where someone has won a title in the Ultimate Fighting Championship with training in only one single style. While world-class MMA professional fighters represent many arts, they all have one thing in common: they know and study Brazilian Jiu-Jitsu! Think about it—from one man's weakness came the most dominant martial art the world has known. If Helio had been born healthy and normal, he would have adapted normally to the Japanese style and never have a need to modify the art. Helio's story has inspired so many martial artists to preserve in hardship. Not only that, but he also created an outlet for many people to learn and train in this wonderful art.

What a story, and what a legacy for a man to leave behind. I'm so glad Helio didn't lie down and accept his "limitations" and submit to his "sickness." He found purpose and value in his tragedy and turned into something great. I'm sure he didn't see the big picture as a sickly sixteen year- old, but he did see something. Maybe a glimmer of hope, maybe a trust in God, maybe he just wouldn't except being down. Whatever it was, I hope each of us can find the same strength and faith young Helio did and discover value in our struggles.

BRIAN

Anybody who has ever done a day on active duty knows that Chad's mindset of being "hurt" rather than "broke" is extremely common among the troops. One of the worst reputations a person can have in the military—at least in the infantry world where I come from—is to be either "that guy" or, even worse, "broke" (and that's putting it nicely).

One of the greatest obstacles faced by a lot of returning combat veterans is trying to get help for an issue they might be dealing with and being worried it will land them in a position where they get known as the guy who is "broke," but not necessarily in the physical sense. I never dealt with this personally. I always performed above average during PT and developed an ability to conceal and put up with a lot of BS. "Suck it up and drive on" is what we say, and that is what I did whenever I had an issue. Back then I would never think of telling my chain of command if I was hurt, unless I was dying, running two miles with a rolled ankle (which I did and it was impossible to hide), or had a fever of 106 (which also happened). Anyone who needs to "talk to the Chaplain" or "go talk to a doctor" instantly has his reputation put on the line. Next thing you know, "PVT Snuffy needs to go to therapy while the rest of us go train for war again…" It's unfortunate, but true. That's just the way it is. Not to mention, in your reputation you could also be "Med-Boarded" out of the military if there is a physical or psychological indication that you may be "unfit for duty." This is especially rough on those who are within five or six years of retirement and fighting to stay in the military to get their pension at twenty years in service—after they've already done fourteen or fifteen years.

There are ways of handling these types of situations on your own without alerting the chain of command in a way that won't set you apart from the crowd or medically put you out of the military. These are simple things you have to think up and do on your own, separate from your time at work in the military. Sometimes you just have to keep things to yourself and let out the stress in other, more productive ways. We will talk more about these things in greater detail in the coming chapters.

To me, being "broke" is more of a state of mind than anything. Of course, some people are physically "broke" and physically unfit for military duty. If you get hurt, you can heal from it in time and get over it. But someone who is "broke" is usually just dead weight for everyone else to carry. I think there are a lot of people who don't give themselves enough credit. They think they are "broke" but they have actually just hit a speed bump along the way and bruised their body or ego and will get over it in time. Everybody gets hurt, but if there is a mission to be completed then sometimes you just have to suck it up and drive on. Life is a mission, and we have to get back up and live it.

CHAPTER 4

THE TRUTH ABOUT
PTSD

BRIAN

One day a close friend presented a great point to me while discussing the topic of Post-Traumatic Stress "Disorder" (PTSD) that has lead me to certain conclusions concerning this particular issue. This man was my first mentor and has likely had a greater impact in my life than any other individual, with the exception of my mother, of course. His comments built on what I had been contemplating for a long time due to my own personal experiences with doctors of many sorts concerning my post-war life.

After coming home combat-wounded from the war in Afghanistan, I was assigned to several doctors, each specializing in his or her own field of medical expertise. More often than not, I would walk into these appointments angry and walk out wanting to shoot something. Talking to these individuals didn't seem to do anything but make me worse. While I sincerely appreciate all they did for me and their sincere efforts to help me put my life back together, but one of the greatest barriers that I faced was the annoying and continual use of the term "disorder"—as in Post-Traumatic Stress "Disorder."

Note to all of the doctors who may be reading this: Thank you for your sincere efforts to help and assist guys like me in putting our lives back together. I truly appreciate you and all of your efforts to help others like me. But if you want to help somebody get better and move beyond their "less than favorable" experiences, do not continually use the term "disorder" as you speak to them.Though calling it as you see it is essential in establishing the reality of where a person may be mentally and emotionally, to continually tell somebody that he or she is "disordered" is no way to help them move beyond their present state.To tell a person they are disordered is to tell them that they are somehow "not normal."The use of this term implies that there is something seriously "wrong" with them, that they are somehow "abnormal." But if this is truly the case, then I would have to ask another question. Does it make an individual "abnormal" if he or she responds in a "normal" manner to a set of "abnormal" circumstances?

If a woman is raped, is she "disorderly" or "abnormal" because she doesn't like to walk down the street alone at night time or be around men she doesn't know? If a man is blown up while at war by a roadside bomb, is he "abnormal" or "disorderly" because he looks for out of place objects that may be lying in the middle of the road or responds to a loud crashing sound? I am not a medical professional and I understand that in many cases, for the sake of maintaining medical insurance coverage for a particular example, it may be necessary to classify such conditions as a "disorder." However, I would advise doctors and other medical professionals to exercise extreme caution in using the term "disorder" when personally addressing those they are trying to help move beyond tragedy and trauma. Are these individuals they are trying to help, these service members and veterans, truly abnormal or disorderly due to their experiences, or are they merely wiser and more in tune with their own survival than many of their counterparts who lack certain life experiences? The person who is on the lookout and constantly prepared for most any situation that might come his or her way is less likely to be taken advantage of and to become a victim of sorts because their responses will be different than of those who are taken by surprise and caught off guard. Their state of being— classified as "abnormal" or "disordered"—in many cases, may actually work to their great advantage and may even contribute to their continued survival.

To date, I've had the honor and privilege of personally mentoring over one-thousand combat veterans from the war on terror in the areas of family, business, life skills (resiliency training), finances, and more. Though every person is different and unique (and some I would classify as "very unique"), there always seems to be a number of common threads among them. For example, I remember talking with a friend of mine who served multiple tours in Iraq and Afghanistan as a Military Police Officer (MP). He worked in the prisons around terrorist detainees all day, every day for months on end. Prior to serving in the military, he worked as a Corrections Officer at one of the "super max" (maximum security) prisons in Colorado, which still houses some of the worst of the worst convicts when it comes to the identities and crimes committed by the inmates. After his military service is complete, he plans to go back to work at that same correctional facility—because he is a Corrections Officer, that's what he does. Several doctors over time have tried to convince him to let go of many of the issues he carries with him, but he simply refuses, and for good reason in some cases. As he and I spoke, I empathized with him as he described to me many of the issues he still carries with him from the war. But at the same time some of those issues are what keep him sharp, and alive, in his dangerous work place environment! Everyday this man works around people who are serving multiple life sentences for their crimes and have absolutely nothing to lose by committing more crimes within the prison walls. I've often heard it said that the most dangerous man in the world is the man who has nothing to lose. I couldn't agree more.

Many of the convicts my friend works around every day are experts at creating small, improvised, homemade weapons, out of seemingly harmless and useless materials that they can and will use to hurt him or somebody else if given the opportunity. It would certainly not be in my friend's best interest to lay down all of the issues he carries with him from his war experience in order to make himself believe that the world is a good place where bad things won't happen simply so he won't have to carry that burden of stress and anger with him every day. Letting his guard down, in this particular case, would not likely work to his advantage. He and I both agreed that this sort of "happy ignorance" is not in our best interest, nor is it in the best interest of those we care about.

My mentor once told me that stress can keep a man sharp and on his toes, but distress can be fatal given the situation. Knowing the difference between the two is imperative. Knowing which issues we need to hang on to and effectively manage for our very survival and safety is crucial. Just as well, knowing which issues to deal with and let go of that will eventually destroy us is equally important. We have to identify and decide what to let go of and when to let go. Timing is everything, but the time to begin this process is now.

CHAD

I often have the enormous privilege to speak in tandem with Dave Roever. When we do, we get up in front of a few thousand people and just be ourselves. We tell our stories and have fun, often taking fun shots to pick at each other. Dave and I always take turns telling the joke: "I don't have PTSD, its PTS." Dave says, "Chad is not disordered, he's just short!" Well, I am a whopping five feet, three inches tall, but you know, if I had to choose, I'd rather be short than "disordered." Dave has a good point, and what I think you will find as the chapter concludes is that combat veterans aren't really disordered. Beyond the comedy of Dave's joke, there is a deep, underlying truth in dropping the "D" from PTSD. In my own experience and in my work with combat veterans, what I have found most disturbing and, unfortunately, most consistent is the prescription of medication to treat the symptoms of PTSD. In many cases we see warriors come into our program on fifteen to twenty scripts JUST FOR PTSD! It is ludicrous! It's a complete numbing of the symptoms so the patient will not have to face the real problem, never have to go through the necessary struggle, and never find healing. You can't be healed if you can't feel! It is a sad and vicious cycle which I hope I can be a part of breaking. Notice the word "symptoms" when you get prescribed medication for PTSD. It is medication for the symptoms of PTSD: anxiety, nightmares, insomnia, etc. Basically, it's an endless cycle of uppers and downers counteracting one another.

When I began to seriously deal with my own PTSD, I had to know that there was more to it than treating symptoms, that there had to be a cure for the root cause. By this time, I had already accepted that Christ was my healing. I knew that no pill, no counseling, no program could replace that. I had also realized that opening myself up and trusting other men to stand alongside me would allow me to continue to heal and grow.

I consider myself a seeker of information. I had a fairly poor and rough life as a child, and I was the first one in my family to go to college. I went into the Marines without even a GED, but with the Corps giving me a fresh shot at life I seized the opportunity and pursued an education. I always looked at education beyond just getting the certificate; I actually loved the knowledge itself. Well, not always. I think a light bulb went off in my first year as a Marine, but I never looked back. After years and years of hard work, I eventually earned my PhD (Doctor of Philosophy) in International Business and my MBA (Masters of Business Administration). I was very proud of earning these degrees, but even with all that knowledge, I had no answers as to what had happened to me and why. So, simply starting to get better was not good enough for me. I had to know and understand what happened to me, and had to know the "why." In my quest for knowledge I discovered two very important things: one, I was not crazy; and two, there were many others like me... too many.

I have always found that working as a formal instructor has been the best way for me to learn. In Jiu-Jitsu I've learned as much if not more from teaching than from being the student. I think it is just a more deliberate and in-depth understanding of the subject. So my path to knowledge led me to complete a thirty credit hour course of study through the American Association of Christian Counselors to be certified as a PTSD Care Provider.

The training was phenomenal. It truly opened my eyes to the "what's" and "whys." of PTSD. One day, I had a class on the physiological effects of trauma and the brain's function in response to trauma. My view of PTSD was changed forever. The knowledge I gained instantly took me to a whole new level of understanding and personal healing. At last, it all made sense!

The Limbic System

I have a great friend, Dr. Richard Wagner. We initially met when I coached him in Jiu-Jitsu, but our friendship grew and we got to know each other on a more personal level. I opened up to him about my PTSD struggles, and he educated me about many of the body's physiological effects. It was always interesting and mutual conversation, since the physiological systems of our bodies and minds are such an intricate part of the martial arts training we have in common. The limbic system was something that I found so fascinating and educational. This knowledge alone was such a powerful part of my healing.

The limbic system is the set of brain structures that forms the inner border of the cortex. (Don't worry; I will keep this in layman's terms for my fellow Marines). It is a part of our brain housing group that sits just above the brain stem and stores historical data. It allows our brain to memorize proper responses to situations we have previously experienced, such as trauma. Typically we reason, think, and make rational decisions in the forebrain. However, if we can condition our brain to respond to a situation instantaneously, that takes place in the limbic system. For example, as warriors we train on the pistol range to respond to a firearm threat. We draw and fire on that threat hundreds of times, so that we won't have to think about it in our forebrain when an actual threat appears. In the forebrain, there would be a delayed decisive response. Because of our training, we are able to see the threat and instantly react, eliminating that bad guy quickly. You see, we store that situation in the limbic system and we can trigger that response off of any of our senses: smell, feel, touch, taste, or sight.

There is one other way that this process happens besides intentionally conditioning our limbic system to work for us—TRAUMA. If we experience a traumatic event, the limbic system immediately stores the event for survival reasons. This process is one of God's little fail-safes in our design. That traumatic event is then stored, regardless of our conscious recollection of it, and our body is prepared to respond to protect itself based on anything that triggers it. Those triggers could be based on any of our senses: smell, feel, touch, taste, or sight. Whatever physiological effects we experienced during the initial incident are stored as a default. If we are triggered, our body immediately goes back to those settings: such as heart rate, adrenaline, vision, audio exclusion, hyper-vigilance, etc.

This explains why the limbic system is most simply known for the four "F's:" fight, flight, feed, and fornicate—all are primal and instinctive properties.

PTSD is commonly defined as the body's normal response to an abnormal situation. Normal response: this means the limbic system's ability to react and ultimately help us survive.

Conclusion: If your history includes you cruising along

Jalalabad Road heading east out of Kabul, Afghanistan and as you drove by a Corolla parked on the left side of the road that some Taliban bugger-eater detonated four rigged 155 rounds he placed in the back seat and then you woke up in Landstuhl Regional Medical Center in Germany...Well, you might chalk that up as a traumatic incident, and don't call yourself crazy when you freak out next time you're in Bails-of-hay, Iowa and you drive past a Corolla parked on the left side of the road. Maybe it's your body trying to keep yourself safe from another explosion. I consider this a great gift that God gave us by design, and knowing this helps just a little bit more to make sense of it all. It also helps me to identify what my triggers are and build boundaries for me and my family to keep me from reacting to them.

There are three categories of PTSD symptoms:

1. Intrusive Memories
2. Avoidance and Numbing
3. Increased Anxiety

1. Intrusive Memories Symptoms:
- Reliving event or flashback
- Nightmares of event

2. Avoidance and Numbing Symptoms:
- Avoid talking or thinking about event
- Feeling emotionally numb
- Avoiding enjoyable activity
- Hopelessness about future

- Memory problems
- Trouble concentrating
- Difficulty maintaining close relationships

3. Increased Anxiety Symptoms:

- Anger or irritability
- Guilt or shame
- Self-destructive behavior
- Dependence on drugs or alcohol
- Trouble sleeping
- Easily startled or frightened
- Hearing or seeing things

These symptoms may come and go. It is important to understand that someone suffering with PTSD may exhibit symptoms from one, two, or all three categories. Most people think that someone with PTSD has to experience all three categories of symptoms. There are also common myths, such as the myth that everyone has flashbacks or nightmares. This is not always true. In many cases, a person may only have one symptom.

CHAPTER 5

ANGLE OF ATTACK

BRIAN

When service members come home from war the last thing on most of their minds is "talking about it." Want to light their fuse? Tell them they need to talk about it. My perspective initially was: "Why talk about it? It is what it is. What happened-happened. It's time to move on." Many people who ask a service member to talk about war do so out of ignorance, that is, they don't always understand what they are asking and in many cases if they were to be told the cold-blooded truth and get the answer they think they want, they would wish they'd never asked.

I know several veterans of past wars who have never talked about their experiences and I understand from my own life experience why they choose not to: difficult emotions, nothing much to talk about, nightmares, flashbacks, or the simple fact that some people simply couldn't handle hearing the explicit, grim, and graphic details concerning the atrocities of war. However, I've also observed some of the long-lasting and damaging effects on the lives of war veterans and their families because these individuals chose never to "talk about it," or at least find an outlet to plug in to.

After returning home from Afghanistan injured, I had no immediate desire to "talk about it." I got so sick and tired of being told to "talk about it," and encouraged to talk about emotions and feelings. "Give me a break, people. Stop trying to be so sentimental," I would think to myself. In fact, many people thought my experience in Afghanistan must have been "very traumatizing," thinking I would sit in a small corner shaking and sweating, not knowing how to handle myself and what I had experienced. It was nothing like that. Everybody handles trauma differently and there is certainly nothing wrong if someone responds to trauma in the manner I just described, but I didn't. My personal response to my own tragic circumstances was a very simple one: "I got blown up by a suicide bomber who exploded about 3-feet away from me. I'm burned 2nd and 3rd degree. It hurt, but I'm still here. It is what it is. The burns will heal. I'll get better." That was pretty much it. So many times, it seemed as if some of my doctors were almost trying to convince me that I should have been reacting differently to my circumstances (and I don't say that proudly or arrogantly). But again, Post-Traumatic Stress is an individual event. Everybody reacts differently to it and there is no less dignity in one reaction than in another. I've simply always been a very practical—and often sarcastic—person, who tries to find humor in everything. I think this has worked to my advantage. For example, while being medevac'd out of Afghanistan and passing through Germany in route to Brooke Army Medical Center in San Antonio, Texas, I had a nurse who was simply doing her job, checking my charts, and she asked me if I had any allergies. I responded to her by saying "I'm allergic to suicide bombers. They're bad for my skin."

You may be thinking, "Wow, Brian. That's pretty sick and twisted." I know, I know, but I had to have some fun with her.

The look on the nurse's face was priceless. That woman didn't know what to do with herself. At first, she laughed, but I put on a stone-face and she quickly caught herself, not knowing if I was joking or being serious. Then I smiled at her and laughed, knowing I had just successfully played a sick joke on her. We had a good laugh together despite the fact I had open 2nd and 3rd degree burns on both of my hands, face, and neck. A little war humor can go a long way!

After coming home, I was asked to talk about things and I didn't feel like there was any point. In some cases, there wasn't. But I can now see how I benefited from it, looking back on those times. At the time I didn't feel it would make any difference and, quite honestly, it didn't on many occasions. After talking about things for fourteen months, I figured if it hadn't helped me by that point then talking about things wasn't going to. What really ended up changing my life for the better wasn't merely "talking about it." It was "how" I talked about it. For example, in my career as an author and speaker I began talking about my experiences with the intention of helping others. This was an entirely different ball game than sitting in some office talking to somebody who may or may not even care whether I live or die.

Only six months following my injury in Afghanistan, I met the man who would become my mentor. A severely injured Vietnam veteran himself, Dave and I had instant credibility with one another. Serving with the Naval Special Forces in Vietnam and poised to throw a white phosphorus hand grenade into a bunker on the bank of the Vam Co Tay River, he was shot by a sniper who was aiming for his head but hit his hand instead. The bullet pierced his hand and the grenade which was only inches from his right ear. In that instant, half of the skin on his body was melted off by the phosphorus. I remember him telling the story graphically:

"I jumped in the water to extinguish the fire but phosphorus burns in water and I could see my skin floating all around me. I was beside myself. I had to pull myself together!"

Wow! What a unique and twisted sense of humor (I loved it!). Here was a man injured in a different war, his injury similar to my own, yet much more severe than mine. Forty years later he had built a highly successful career as an author and speaker and was having fun and doing something constructive with all of the pain he once endured. Surely, I thought, if this guy can get through what he went through, then I can do something with my own situation. That thought was a major key to my success, by the way. There was hope.

About a month later I received a call from his office asking me to come and be a part of a patriotic rally he was speaking at near Fort Reilly, Kansas. The lady on the phone told me the trip would be free and that they would cover all of my expenses. Free is good, so I took full advantage of the opportunity. What they failed to tell me, however, is that there would be over 3,000 people in the audience at the event! Not knowing what to say, I simply stated my name, who I served with, what happened to me, and that I thought perhaps I was still alive for a reason. It was nothing that I would consider "inspirational" by my own standard.

However, after I was done talking, a young lady who was in her early twenties approached me. She began telling me about some of the hardships she had endured in her own life. Then she tagged the following statement on the end of our conversation (and this is what I call "The Game Changer"):

"But if you can get through all of that, then I think I can also get through what I'm going through."

From that moment on, my life has never been the same. It was in that moment, for the first time since my tragic and painful war injury, that I felt I had begun finding a purpose for my injury. All of a sudden my war injury had become purpose-driven. At that point, there was a glimmer of hope that perhaps there was a greater reason, beyond me, for everything that was happening. I had always believed that there was a greater purpose for my injury—at least, I had held out hope that there was. Now, just six months later, I was beginning to see my hopes and prayers answered. Those answers came only through serving others by talking about what had happened to me. What happens to you in life isn't nearly as important as what you choose to do with what happens to you in life.

And that's the truth. When you take the focus of your experiences off of yourself and begin using those experiences to focus on, help and serve other people, your life will change dramatically for the better. I've never lived a better life since almost losing it while fighting the war in Afghanistan. At this point I wouldn't go back in time and change anything that happened to me in Afghanistan even if I had the chance. The reason I can make such a statement is because of all of the positive impact I've been able to have in the lives of thousands of people during my live events and the influence I've been able to spread by getting my message out in front of millions more through national and international television and radio broadcasts, national publications, and other media outlets. All of that good has taken place as a result of the bad that happened to me in Afghanistan. Every evil thing that suicide bomber had intended to accomplish through attacking me has been turned completely in another direction and is now accomplishing everything, and more, that he intended to destroy. Additionally, the suicide bomber was the only one to die that day. Funny? No. Hilarious? Yes! Mission Accomplished? Sure! That suicide bomber went into Kandahar to die that day and that is exactly what he did. All the suicide bomber ended up really doing was handing me a great life and a great career on a silver platter that now helps other guys just like me and he didn't even know it. Funny how life works out sometimes.

I still find it hard to believe sometimes that I get to go to the places I go, meet the people I meet, and do what I do all over the globe—all because something bad happened to me and it's now being used for good. That is something I certainly never could have planned on my own. This is only one, of many, reasons that I know and believe that there is a greater purpose for my life. Simply "talking about it" wasn't what made the difference in my life. Again, it was "how" I chose to talk about my experiences and what I chose to do with them that changed everything. Regardless of your life's circumstances, I know that the same can be true in your life as well. I know there is a greater purpose and a greater plan for your life and mine beyond what we can presently see and I believe it is our job to search it out and find it. I believe that my purpose in life is to help you find yours. If I die having accomplished at least that much, then I will have died a happy and satisfied man.

If you have no desire to talk about your experiences, then don't! With some people, the more you push them to do something they don't want to do the more you will push them away and build up an impenetrable resistance. But I would also highly discourage you from holding that position as a permanent one. If you can find other means by which you can release those things in some way, shape or form, then do it. In the following chapters, I will be revealing other productive habits I've personally adopted and benefited from that have allowed me to move beyond certain post-war experiences when nothing else was working.

CHAD

There are so many stories that come to mind to validate what Brian is saying here. Sure, we all learn and grow from our own struggles and pitfalls, but so can others. The value in our stories and experiences can be so powerful to others when shared with an authentic and open heart. But, we will never know *how* powerful unless we can make ourselves available and vulnerable to do so.

This story of Alex, a friend and fellow Marine who I worked with at Mighty Oaks, is one of my all-time favorites.

Alex was out with another Marine in our program, passing out info at a booth outside a Wal-Mart in Salida, Colorado, population: 5,000. An older gentleman stopped to offer a donation. They asked him if he had received a flyer on the way into the store. He said no, but he supported the troops in any way he could. Alex handed him a flyer and started talking to him about our programs and what we do to help our warriors. The man began to tell them about his grandson who served in the Marines in Iraq. Since the two men working the table were Marines, there was a moment of excitement. Alex told the man how they both served in the Marines in Iraq as well, and asked him who his grandson had served with in the Marine Corps, to which the man responded, "3/1," meaning 3rd Battalion / 1st Marines. With surprise, Alex then let him know he had also served in 3/1.

Alex then asked, "What company?" and the man told him "Lima Company." The man added, "My grandson was killed in Fallujah."

"Sir, I fought in that battle," Alex exclaimed. He went on to tell a story he felt compelled to share with the man: "I was there going door to door through that city. I remember being called to support Lima Company because they were pinned down by a sniper. By the time we got there for support, one of their Marines had been shot. I helped carry him and then passed him off to my friend because I kept falling in the rubble. I continued as security while my friend continued to carry him until we got to the Humvees. Once there, the corpsmen declared him KIA (killed in action). This Marine had been shot by a sniper, and the bullet entered his neck and came out right beneath the back of his skull."

The man looked at Alex with a blank stare and then said, "That was exactly the same way my grandson was killed." Alex and the man stared at each other for a little while. Then he told the man he never knew the Marine's name and wasn't insinuating this was his grandson. But, the similarity in their stories was uncanny considering the small window of time in the two-week battle of Fallujah for the Marines, and they both knew. Alex went on to tell the man that, later that day, he had engaged in the battle, and that he had shot and killed the enemy sniper who had killed the young Marine. Alex and I spent a lot of time thinking about the likelihood of the same story happening to two different Marines from the same Battalion, same Company, and at the same place in the same battle. Highly unlikely! In the small town of Salida, Colorado, did God send Alex to give this grandfather the story of his grandson's death? Maybe that man got the peace he needed, in meeting the Marine who had held his dying grandson, and avenged his death by taking out his killer. He was maybe finally able to lie to rest a grandson, a United States Marine, who sacrificed his life for this great nation in the face of evil.

You cannot image how on top of the world Alex felt. I saw him come to life, knowing that his story had touched the life of someone in pain. It was so clear that Alex's story helped to heal a wound in this grandfather's life that might otherwise have lasted forever. We never know the power of our stories, the value in our experience, and the joy in using them to serve others.

CHAPTER 6

PULLING THE TRIGGERS

BRIAN

Triggers are everywhere, not only on our firearms. Triggers exist in almost every realm of life: from weaponry, marketing, and the aerospace industry to the full spectrum of human emotion. A trigger acts offensively. Just pull one and you'll find out! Pulling a trigger is a simple enough act, but the ramifications and outcome of the pulling of a trigger can permanently change the world as we know it for better or for worse. When pulled, it instigates a situation and demands a reaction. It always causes a reaction when pulled. For example, a smooth-talking salesman who is exceptionally good at his job could virtually sell ice cubes to an Eskimo in the middle of a snowstorm through the use of triggers; psychological triggers, in this case. By using the right words and identifying key aspects of importance in the other man's life and then proceeding to identify a concrete reason that those ice cubes are essential to either survival, the avoidance of great pain, or to a continued way of life, the salesman is in the beginning phase of pulling triggers in the mind of his prospect. The salesman could also tell the man that the ice cubes he is selling are in limited supply and only available for a very short period of time and are selling fast. Of course, if the salesman offers to throw in a free, highly-valuable and much needed bonus as a part of the deal that the other man gets only if he buys from him at that moment, the salesman is very likely to make the sale. The reason for this is obvious. The salesman did his homework on his prospect. He identified triggers of great importance that pertained to his prospect, and then he simply began pulling those triggers in sequence. He identified a want or need, added great value, created scarcity, and then presented his product as the solution to the other man's need while adding a limited-time bonus (a bonus too good to turn down) to make the prospect want his product right then and there. Choosing to greatly discount the price of the item while topping it off with a rock solid money-back guarantee... SOLD! The salesman more than likely made the sale simply because he identified the triggers and chose which ones to push and which ones not to push. While the above example could be true in a sales and marketing situation, the concept of identifying and knowing what triggers are and how they work is essential to your continued success in most, if not every, aspect of your life. Have you ever known somebody who knew just the right buttons to push, and in which order, to make you angry? That person was intentionally pulling certain triggers in order to provoke a particular response out of you. However, there are also times in life when our triggers get pulled unintentionally, whether by a person or random circumstance, and to those around us it can be very obvious that something just happened. This can be a somewhat common scenario among returning combat veterans. The good news, however, is that you and I have the ability to choose and even alternate the outcome when certain triggers in our lives get pulled. It's not always easy and it can definitely take practice and time, but it is crucial that we each identify these alternate solutions in our own lives.

Certain triggers in military service members and combat veterans vary across a wide range of issues and scenarios. One person may see somebody who resembles a terrorist wearing a burka or middle eastern garb and have a trigger get pulled while another is triggered by the memory of the smell of a blown up and burning vehicle they were inside of in Afghanistan, which could easily happen while driving past the scene of a car accident back home. From gun shots at a rifle range to situations that remind a person of life at war, these are just a few common examples of triggers that exist in the lives of military service members and veterans. When these triggers get pulled, it's vital to have already begun identifying our own individual "Release Valves," which we will discuss in the next chapter.

CHAD

Military guys do stupid stuff as it is; add PTSD and drugs or alcohol to the mix and we are just asking for trouble. Identifying your triggers is important, and learning to put boundaries in place to keep you from being triggered is vital. If you are out of the military or in the process of getting out, it is imperative that you come to grips and realize you are not in the military anymore. The civilian world is not a big team, and certain behavior that was unacceptable but tolerable in the military, is truly unacceptable in the civilian world, "!" exclamation point. Trust me; I've hit the punch line on a few jokes that only resulted in dropped jaws and blank stares. It's embarrassing—don't go there.

As a military guy, especially as a Marine, I can remember so many times being part of or witnessing my fellow Marines doing the most idiotic stuff, mostly out of boredom. I remember one night when I was much younger I was living in the barracks in 29 Palms, California and me and some of my Recon Teammates and I were enjoying a movie and drinking beer. I honestly never was a beer drinker, or big on any alcohol; however, I used to think it was pretty hysterical to watch what would happen when bored Marines would drink beer in the barracks. Despite my present day ministerial status, I will confess that at that time in my life this was entertainment to me. This particular night would not be a disappointment, as my drunken Marine brothers would deliver! We were watching a movie that I'm sure you've seen: *Point Break,* starring Keanu Reeves. It was Melton, Ohlson, Terrell and I. As a surprise to us, Ohlson had invited a Marine from another unit. . . . Never a good idea! You see, for those who haven't served, here is how it works. If there is a multiple country service around, then the U. S. Military stands together. If it is only the U. S. Military, then there is surely service to service rivalry. If there are Marine tankers and infantry around, there is a feud brewing, and heaven forbid multiple Infantry Platoons in an armory cleaning weapons together...There will be a fist fight. You see, competition is so embedded there must be a rival, and that means someone has to be the odd man out.

This poor guy came into our barracks and somehow started an argument over Keanu Reeves' wingman. Was it Nick Nolte or Gary Busey? Terrell made it clear that it was Nolte with a right cross to the poor guy's face, and it was on. As Terrell and this guy were fighting, I was getting my dose of Friday night entertainment when all of a sudden Melton decided to jump in by coming off the top rack of the bunks with a Jimmy Superfly Snuka elbow to the head of the guy who said it was Busey. Turns out it really was Busey, but who cares? You don't need a valid reason to go WWE during a good barracks fight. Fortunately, no Marines were injured during the making of this story, and I know Terrell and the other Marine would fight side by side against a common enemy, but the point is...What was the point?!?! I just wanted to add in a good story and tell you: Don't go drinking in the barracks and flying off the top rack like a WWE Superstar.

Seriously, military guys get used to doing goofy stuff. It is the norm. Military life is different, and contrary to how normal this story may seem to you, this behavior would not be acceptable on a corporate business trip with your co-workers.

Making the integration into the civilian world is tough enough, and doing it with PTSD is even tougher. In identifying your triggers, you have to develop boundaries and parameters to prevent them from being set off.

Remember when I talked about the limbic system? I described how it stores historical data so that the brain can memorize proper responses to situations we previously experienced, such as our personal traumatic experiences. When we operate in our limbic part of the brain, we don't think with reason here; we don't make rational decisions here. However, when we trigger our PTSD this is where we are. And you don't belong there when you are trying to tuck your kids in at night. You don't want to be in the same physiological state of operation as leading soldiers in combat when your little girl takes too long to put on her shoes.

You see, we store that situation in the limbic system and we can trigger that response off of any of our senses: smell, feel, touch, taste, or sight. We have to learn what things set us off, and our spouses have to know too. And spouses, please don't think it's a good idea to use them as buttons to push when you are mad and vengeful. It might not turn out the way you want.

My wife and I have figured out a lot of things that provoke my moods and emotions, but I still get blindsided from time to time. Just a few weeks ago, I had a sobering reminder of triggers and an unexpected recollection of events that I struggle with.

I work with other combat veterans full time. I'm supposed to be a model of someone healed. And I often boast in my recovery, when in programs with other veterans or in public arenas. I boast of how I am a successful product of healing.

After a week of working with a group of Marines in one of our programs, I had a harsh reminder of the fact that although I may not have PTSD anymore, I have been through a struggle and will have to live with those experiences. The Fight Club program had just graduated and, after a long week, I went to the movies with my two boys. Kathy and my teenage daughter had dropped us off to go shopping. We live about an hour and a half from a big grocery store. So, Kathy has it figured out that it is cheaper to drop me and the boys off at a movie than to take us shopping. She's smart to save the money and we get to see a movie, one of my favorite things to do.

I have seen lots of war and combat movies since I've dealt with PTSD and none have really affected me at all. However, this particular movie had a scene in it that struck so close to home it could have been a reenactment. I'm sitting there and I notice my heart beating fast, and my breathing increase. I think, "Oh my God, I know what this is, a panic attack, and I can't believe it's happing to me." My ego was reminding me, "You just helped eighteen Marines with this; you can't be facing this still." But I was. My arms and face started going numb and I could hardly breathe. As I was getting out of there, boys in tow, I could hear my sixteen-year-old asking me if I was okay. I sat down and just broke into tears.

Kathy had just driven by to pick us up and when she saw me, she left the car in the parking lot. She ran over and held me; of course, this made me cry more. I was bawling uncontrollably and didn't know why. I never can put a finger on the "whys" but the symptoms are always the same, and it had been a long time. None the less there I was, in front of a few hundred people coming out of Cinemark, all probably wondering if my dog just died.

I called Dave Roever and talked to him about it, and he told me how sorry he was that this had happened. However, I replied that I wasn't sorry; I was happy and accepting of it. It was my past and a good reminder of where I was, where I am, and where the warriors we help may be. I was able to identify another trigger that day and put another boundary in my life to help continue my process of healing.

CHAPTER 7

RELEASE VALVES

BRIAN

Commit to finding solutions that won't land you in jail! Know yourself and continually learn more about yourself. Stop sitting around doing nothing and educate yourself if you're not already doing so. Seek as much formal education as you possibly can while pursuing a personal journey of self-education (education that comes from outside of the classroom). Know what motivates you. What makes you angry? What makes you happy or excited? What allows you to blow off steam and simply be yourself? What makes you feel relaxed?

Knowing the answers to these questions may seem menial at first glance, but the consequences and ramifications of not knowing the answers to these questions will become more than evident the longer you continue to live without certain knowledge.

I remember watching the movie *Rudy* when I was a kid. You've more than likely seen the movie multiple times. It's the story of a kid whose dream is to play football for the University of Notre Dame in South Bend, Indiana. The only problem is that Rudy comes from a poor family, he is too small, his grades are terrible… You name it, the odds were against him. Although Rudy did end up accomplishing his goal in the end, it didn't come without sacrifice and loss. Not only did he give up a lot of things in life to reach his goal, but he also lost his best friend to a work-related accident. If you've seen the movie recently, you'll remember the giant tank that exploded in the factory in which Rudy and his best friend worked. The tank of compressed gas became too full and eventually it became dangerously unstable. It kept filling and filling and filling and they were unable to let the pressure out in time. Consequently, the tank exploded into a giant ball of fire. His friend was killed in the explosion. He became collateral damage. It was the loss of his friend that pushed Rudy over the edge to pursue a goal everyone told him was both stupid and impossible and had never been done by a person of his stature and status.

We all have times when we have to let off some steam. The trick is finding an effective way of doing so without going to jail. Ideally, it wouldn't be in a public location after an extended period of time of bottling up a bunch of repressed thoughts and memories from, or caused by, war. Preferably, it wouldn't be drug or alcohol related. So often everything appears absolutely fine on the outside, until one day a person seems to randomly explode and completely goes off the deep end, leaving everybody else standing around asking the question, "What's his problem?"

Each one of us has a certain number of release valves. Some of the people you see on TV getting arrested or read about in the newspaper, unfortunately, haven't identified theirs and end up paying dearly for it, in many cases.

Every person has at least two or three primary release valves, some have more. But what may work for one person may not work for another because everybody is different. It is your responsibility to find what works for you and then use them as outlets when necessary.

Need a real-life example? I'll use myself as one here. I have figured out what some of my own primary release valves are and trust me when I say I am forced to use them often. After speaking in as many prisons as I have over the course of my career as an author and speaker, I know that there are few things in life, if any, worth going to prison over. When I get angry, frustrated, or uptight about something or somebody, I go for a motorcycle ride. I ride with no destination in mind and with no time limits or concerns. I don't care who doesn't know where I'm going or when I'll be back or who doesn't like it because I ride until I feel better, period. It sure beats the alternative of being criminally charged for domestic violence, or worse! Remember men, anything beats a domestic violence charge! Other times I work out at the gym until I'm too physically exhausted to care anymore, or do Krav Maga (a hand-to-hand combat system developed by the Israel Defense Forces-its great stuff).

Additionally, I bought a dog. I have a German Shepherd named Maverick who weighs well over 100 pounds. I had him professionally trained in home protection and to attack on command. I continually work with him and training him is a great way to relieve stress. Even still, there are times I'll hike out into the mountains in the middle of nowhere, turn off my cell phone (which provides a little-known sense of freedom), listen to some of my favorite public speakers talk, escape to the solitude of my travel trailer and listen to music as I work on a project or write (I know, I'm officially a nerd now... but it works). Remember, the goal here is to be able to let off steam without going to jail.

On the flip side, I would highly suggest not implementing methods for relieving stress that have the ability to alter or distort your mind or mood, such as through the use of alcohol (aka- "liquid courage that makes me bulletproof") or drugs of that sort. I KNOW, I KNOW... You can't believe a combat-infantryman like me would say such a thing. Its borderline blasphemous, I know. To tell somebody in the military not to use alcohol as a means to an end seems ridiculous, especially given the number of people in the military who drink alcohol like kids drink fruit punch. But if something takes you out of control of your own mind, even if temporarily, then you also have to be ready for a reality check because unfortunately you are still responsible for yourself, even if you happen to become less than "coherent" for any good or bad reason.

If you don't identify the release valves in your own life and you end up doing something that either you or somebody else will regret, sadly there will be nobody to blame but yourself and no excuse good enough to get you out of the situation.

One great example of this was the time I met the first person I'd ever known who had apparently been criminally charged with "mayhem." He's now become a friend of mine. At the time, I had no idea what constituted "mayhem." But according to some of my sources, I later learned that "mayhem" is apparently a lot like "assault," except somebody loses a body part! My friend was fully intact after the fight was over. In the end, both he and the other guy paid a hefty price for the altercation. Although this particular friend is one of those guys who is nothing but fun to be around and can make just about anybody laugh, he had made a decision that greatly impacted his life, as well as the lives of those close to him.

Identify your own methods for dealing with the issues of life according to your own personal likes and interests. If you do this, you'll likely be much happier, stay married longer, and not end up in jail (remember, this was part of our goal)!

Replacement Conditioning

He was 6 ft. 5 in. tall. He weighed nearly four hundred pounds. He played in the Super Bowl, wrestled professionally for decades, and has been a pro athlete for nearly forty years. I walked into the gym to find my friend, a giant boulder of a human being, on the floor doing the splits. Even in his fifties he was still able to do this, and then lean forward and touch his face to the ground at the same time. His peak physical condition was beyond impressive.

I've always said that smart people understand the value of hanging out with those who are further along and much older.

In my life, I've benefitted in ways I could have never imagined by doing so. Some things can only be learned through personal experience, but as I previously mentioned it can be extremely beneficial to learn from somebody else's experiences.

My friend taught me a lesson that day that changed my life forever. As we spoke, he began referring back to the days when he was "in his prime." Though still very active and very successful, he taught me a lesson from his own life that has greatly impacted me.

(Note: One of the greatest habits I've developed is to identify where others are strong in their lives and then take their lessons and apply them to mine. Doing so has made me a better, stronger, more successful person in every way).

My friend humbly admitted to me that for a time in his life much of his success went to his head in that he was so physically large and strong that practically no human being could take him one-on-one. He was huge and he was strong and he knew it. In the sports he played, he was a wrecking ball of a man. Today he is one of the most down-to-earth and sincere people I know. His life experience has brought him to the place he is now and has shaped him into the man he is today. Still very active and still very strong, he is a more wellrounded man than he had been previously.

He and I were in deep conversation when he began telling me about his past drug and alcohol addiction. He recalled how he would be up all hours of the night and continually fall into the temptation of driving to the liquor store at two or three o'clock in the morning and meet up with a guy who would get him "the stuff" he so desperately craved. After years of making this a habit, he found this vicious cycle to be something almost impossible to break and it was destroying his life. After a failed suicide attempt, everything changed.

"Replacement therapy," as he called it, was one of his keys to recovering from his addictions and moving forward in life again. It helped him turn his life completely around. I prefer to dub this concept *"Replacement Conditioning,"* simply due to the fact that many people associate failure and other things they don't want to admit with the term "therapy." To some, especially those of us in the military, the term "therapy" implies weakness— something we are taught from day one to never show or admit. Conditioning, however, is the action one takes in order to begin preparing for a challenge or undertaking, especially an athletic one.

Night after night, my friend began replacing his night-time rendezvous with a few key pieces of equipment from his gym. He had dumbbells, an exercise ball, and flex hoses. He would put them on the floor of his bedroom or living room and begin doing simple exercises. He would do various exercises, one after the other, consistently, until he worked completely through his set and was physically drained. That's it!

My friend found something else, something productive, to help him replace the things in his life that were ultimately destroying him and holding him back. Experts over the years have claimed it takes about twenty one days to develop a new habit and get rid of an old one. As with any new habit or undertaking, the first few days to a week are the most difficult to stay consistent. Accountability to another person is essential. But when you begin replacing certain destructive habits in your life, or medicines with varying side effects that could cost you dearly in the long run, you will begin to discover that oftentimes there are several activities of daily life that you can do in order to assist in replacing certain bad habits or even medicine you may be taking. I've been told by numerous medical professionals that there are several activities in which a person can become involved in that can cause the brain to begin releasing some of the same types of chemicals that many medicines do to help a person to feel better and more balanced physically, mentally, and emotionally. The big benefit of participating in such activities is that the effects are all natural. There are no heavy side effects to these alternatives practices because they don't involve any prefabricated or manufactured drugs.

I WANT TO BE VERY CLEAR that I am not advising anybody to stop taking any medications they are presently being prescribed. Doing so could be very harmful, even fatal, in some situations. Always be sure to consult with a medical professional before altering your medical dosages or choosing to come off of medication completely. Much of the time that I discuss this topic with service members and veterans, I am more often than not addressing those who are being prescribed large doses of psychotropic drugs.

My opinion here is a simple one: to live a better life, take only medications you absolutely need and if you are able to replace certain medications with varying activities of daily life in order to get a similar, or better, effect than that which the medicine gives you, then I would recommend trying to do so. I am a huge fan of modern medicine and what it has the ability to do for the human race in helping us to live better lives. However, I am also a firm believer that there is not a pill for every problem known to man, nor should we live and pretend as if this is the case. No matter how badly we would like this to be true there is not a pill for everything, therefore we must seek alternate solutions to make up for where medicines fail, fall short, and cannot suffice.

In many of my personal experiences, medicine was nothing more than a temporary solution to a problem that required permanent closure. At times, certain pills and medications were nothing more than band aids on a hemorrhaging wound. For a time, these solutions may be the only ones offered to us and we would be crazy not to try any pill that could help solve a problem. The biggest problem with pills, however, comes when one of them either begins having a negative side effect on our mind or body or when our bodies begin building up a tolerance to a particular substance. It is at this point that doctors usually begin prescribing more and more medicines to their patients not because they have a rapidly increasing condition, but rather to counter the effects of another medicine in our system. Before you know it, a person has gone from taking one or two pills every day to taking fifteen or twenty pills a day. I've watched person after person become a victim of this vicious cycle and the lifestyle they live is one I wouldn't wish on anybody.

I came to this point at a time in my life as well and I chose to fight it head-on or die trying. I simply refused to live the rest of my life as a zombie due to the numerous side effects of several pills. I figured that at least if I were angry or frustrated over something, it was really me who was angry and frustrated, not just some alternate version of me who was ignorantly blissful because of some alternating level of artificial chemicals in my brain. After making this decision, I realized I still had battles to fight and it was imperative for me to begin discovering and developing alternate means of dealing with certain issues. It was then that my friend's concept of *"Replacement Conditioning"* rose to a position of prominence in my own life and began taking me in a new direction.

First, I had to identify the triggers that activated certain issues in my life. Then, I had to identify my "release valves." Once I uncovered and began implementing this strategy, my daily life became more like a basketball game, a continual "action and reaction" sequence of events…And the ball was in my court!

CHAD

I can remember when I first came home and was diagnosed with PTSD. I had absolutely no idea what PTSD was; in fact, when my doctor told me I had PTSD, I was relieved. I thought, *Yea Man, nothing is wrong with me; I'm not losing my mind. I'll just get a shot, hop a flight back across the pond, and be back to work.* I thought PTSD was something I had caught from eating the local food or something. But to find out I had Post-Traumatic Stress Disorder was an affirmation of my fears. I can remember the panic and fear of losing my mind, and physically I felt like my body would literally stop working. The physical effects of the panic attacks made me feel like I was having a heart attack and my throat was swelling shut. So, to do any type of physical fitness for therapy had me in fear that I would just fall over and die. It was a very hopeless feeling.

As I mentioned in Chapter 2, I have been a lifelong martial artist. Rediscovering the martial arts has been one of my main "release valves". What I have found is that, when I'm grappling or wrestling, I can't think of anything else. I have to be in the present moment. If you have ever wrestled or grappled, you'll be able to relate to this. I've found that if my mind starts to wander, my training partner will be all over me, and will choke me out. Getting back into grappling, I had to stay engaged and it felt good to finally have focus again.

There are some other benefits, as well. The camaraderie of being part of a team again, for example, and hanging out with the boys. I have never been one to frequent a bar or pool hall. If you are, please don't misunderstand my "hanging out with the boys" comment for a green light to hit the local pub till two in the morning and tell war stories over a few pints. My personal opinion of that scenario is that it's a recipe for disaster. First of all, PTSD and alcohol do not mix. Second, the average drunken idiots you find in a pub and combat vets do not mix. And lastly, you telling your war stories in a public place typically invites a challenge from one of those idiots and somebody ends up going to jail—probably the crazy veteran. Stay in safe places with people who care about you. That's the kind of camaraderie I found on the mats. I made good friends there, even non-military guys—yes, we can be friends with civilians too. You'll learn as you become a civilian again that there really are some great people out there. This country we fought for is not just a country of sheep that we served as sheep dogs. Some of my best friends today are men and women who never served and it has been a huge joy to have opened that door in my life.

Another thing I found on the mats—and in fitness training in general—is the euphoric effect you feel after a workout. If you are not a fitness guru, I am not talking about during the workout, but after it, when the endorphins are released in your body. You just feel better, not only physically but—even more importantly—mentally and emotionally. This makes exercise a great release valve.

So often, when we face anxiety and stress, we run to a pill bottle for that script or maybe a little beyond. Maybe we hit the fridge for a beer or two or ten, get on a motorcycle and go 120 mph down the freeway, quit our job, act out in road rage, or snap at the ones closest to us, such as our spouse or our kids. If any of these scenarios hit close to home, then I challenge you to try "replacement conditioning." Regardless of whether you think these behaviors are normal or not, let me tell you... they are not. And guess what else? Everyone else besides you is not an idiot.

Sometimes you need to recognize when you are getting worked up and change your behavior by doing something productive. You need to find that physical outlet, replace that negative behavior with positive physical behavior and get some endorphins released in your body. Watch how differently you will not only feel but also behave. And dog-ear this page for the other thing I'm about to say. Highlight it and share it with your spouse.

SPOUSES, you want a better husband or wife at home? You have to give them this time. It is more important than any therapy.

There is a couple I have worked with at Eagles Summit Ranch. The husband is an Army sniper, a phenomenal man with a great family. He has done really well in recovering from PTSD and is now helping many others. He got into downhill mountain biking for the same reasons as I do Jiu-Jitsu. He says that if he isn't one-hundred percent focused on his bike and path, he will end up going over the side of a cliff or crash into a rock. He found peace and focus in this outlet, a brotherhood of guys and, I'm certain, a huge release of endorphins to calm anxiety and stress. All of these factors have helped to balance his life. He has done well with it and is even sponsored now. I'm sure his wife has many days away from him when he's out on the mountain and wishes he was home with the family. Many spouses would try to put a stop to activities like this, but productive and necessary outlets bring balance and peace back into the home. But the thing is, if this soldier weren't on that bike racing down the mountain, his family might not be doing as well as it is. Spouses, support and encourage your warrior; giving a little on your end could very well produce the result you are so desperately seeking.

Chapter 8

No Entitlements

CHAD

There is a reason communist and socialist societies have never survived. It's because motivation and success are based on personal buy-in. To be a part of the solution and not a product of the solution is what keeps self-worth alive. I remember when Hurricane Katrina hit New Orleans, Louisiana and everyone was complaining about the federal government's response. There was a New Orleans resident on the Houston news (a lot of the refugees went to Houston). He was throwing a fit about his cash cards not being enough, and he made this comment: "If you can't depend on your government, then who can you depend on?" I wanted to jump through the screen, give him a good shaking, and give him the answer: "Yourself! Depend on yourself, man!!!" What makes undeserving people feel entitled to depend on others for help or handouts?

I personally don't want a handout because I got sick, and I don't want to see my brothers trade their character and dignity for something they don't deserve. The rules are pretty simple: get the help you need, and have some integrity about it, too. Don't take advantage of a system just because it's easy to. There are pay and recovery programs in place for a reason. If you got hurt in the line of your duty, then by all means use them. Getting the help you need is not what I'm criticizing here. Becoming dependent on a system is.

You can't depend on a system to take care of you, or you'll set yourself up for failure. You have to take leadership in your recovery, and set a goal to get out of the process instead of becoming a permanent resident of it. This requires goals: short-term and long-term. You can't get anywhere if you don't know where you're going, and you can't grab the future if you're holding onto the past. Lean forward. If you lean forward and you fall...well, you'll fall forward!

Put that goal on a map and head for it. Government or program help should only be pit stops on your path to recovery.

Caution-Caution on many of these vet pet programs. Everyone wants to jump on the "wounded veteran/soldier/warrior" bandwagon and it's sad! Some people want you on a poster or a TV ad; they want your story to attach to their program. Why? For money, and not money for you! And some vets will sell themselves for a horseback ride or fishing trip. There are some great programs out there. America loves their warriors. Look for programs that invest in your lasting recovery, or are interested in including your family—not just a good time for a weekend.

It's not about enabling; it's about lifting each other up. It is okay to take a hand when you're down. Just be willing to let it go when you're up and on your feet—you will need that hand to lift up the next guy.

In 1999, I went to the U.S. Army Special Forces Military Free-Fall School at Ft. Bragg, NC, also known as HALO School for

High Altitude Low Opening. During the training you travel to Yuma, Arizona, where you do thirty or so free-fall skydives with combat equipment from heights exceeding 30,000 feet. It's awesome training. People always ask me, why I would jump out of a perfectly good airplane? Well, for one, I truly loved it; and two, the military doesn't have many perfectly good airplanes so I was glad to jump out of them. The most amazing thing, though, is that after only a week of training in a free-fall simulator—a wind tunnel at Ft. Bragg—we were going to just get into a plane and jump out with an instructor. Not attached, but just free-falling alongside of you for evaluation and help if needed. I think back to how trusting I and the other students were in a group of instructors we had never met before. I had no idea who this man was, but was literally going to step out into the abyss of the sky and trust that he would see me to safety. You see, I didn't have to know him; I had to know where he came from. All the instructors were from my military community, and they were all brothers. I knew who he was even without knowing him, and I knew without question that I could trust him with my life.

As combat veterans we often feel alone. No one can be trusted to help us. Yet, we are part of a team, a brotherhood of those we can trust and lean on. What a bonus! Don't ever let go of that camaraderie, that band of brothers.

BRIAN

'Nuff said!

CHAPTER 9

BATTLE-HARDENED

CHAD

This is a chapter for the spouses, family members, and friends of combat veterans. In working with families, I often hear, "He's not the same person he used to be before he deployed." Well, no kidding! Of course he's not—he just went to war! How could anyone be the same after doing and seeing the things war exposes you to? I would be more concerned about a person who did come back the same. When I hear spouses say this I generally reply, "What the heck did you think you were signing up for?" Either you married into the military or you likely chose, as a couple, to join the military.

A commitment to serve our country as a warrior spouse is no different than that of the warrior, and it is equally demanding post-war. So many spouses want to give up when their warrior needs them most. In sickness and in health, sound familiar? Well, PTSD is a sickness! My hat is off to the wives and husbands who understand this. They are some of the greatest American heroes in this war. We need more of you!

I know that my wife went through her own war with my deployments and my recovery. I'm so grateful for her strength when I was weak. Now I can be strong for her again, but she had her season to rise up and take the lead for a while when our family needed it most.

One common problem that can come up is that after the warrior has gotten better, they have become too comfortable with the role of the spouse taking over and they allow it to stay that way. Men, lead your homes. If your wife took over while you got your stuff together, great—but take your role back. As much as you both may be thinking that she doesn't want you to—trust me, she wants you to! I've heard husbands say, "She won't let me take over now; she's so dominant." You show me a dominant woman, and I'll show you a weak man who is not leading. A family needs a leader, and if the man won't be that leader, then the woman will typically step up, and life isn't fun in that house for anyone. So get it straight, men.

Bottom line is this: the warrior and the spouse or family member or friends have to align as a team and fight together. You cannot put this struggle between you and make the fight amongst yourselves. Treat it like a common enemy. In every single battle you face, step back and figure out how you can face it together.

Realizing you are not each other's enemy is the key element to winning the war at home.

BRIAN

Chad hit the nail on the head in that last paragraph. If more service members and spouses treated the post-war battles they face like the common enemies they are and fought together in the same way that our fire teams and platoons fight terrorists, there would be a lot less collateral damage after coming home from war, especially when it comes to divorce.

I know that there have been times when my wife and I have gotten into heated arguments brought on, more often than not, by a PTSD-related issue. As we began talking and discussing the issues strategically and trying to work together in a more rational way, we typically found that "each other" wasn't the issue. Usually, I had something else on my mind troubling me or frustrating me and Jamie and/or the kids were simply the ones who were in the line of fire when the trigger got pulled.

What do you do when you're being shot at? You shoot back! What do you think my wife would do when she would get caught in the crossfire? Yes, that's right. She would shoot back. Now, instead of being a team that can fight our common enemy together head-on and devise strategies for defeating it, we had turned our sights on each other. This is very common in military marriages. It's no wonder the divorce rate in the military is astronomical. We get home from literally getting shot at, only to be verbally assaulted and shot at in our own homes—and sometimes we instigated the fight!

The previous book I wrote about my personal war experience in Afghanistan is entitled *Never the Same*, and for good reason. It's like Chad said earlier: "Of course he is different; of course he's not the same. He went to war!"

It is possible to turn the crosshairs from pointing at each other to pointing at your common enemy (PTSD, Anxiety, Anger,

TBI, you name it). For the most effective changes in your life to take place concerning these issues and those like them, it doesn't usually require long, giant, dramatic steps to be taken suddenly and all at once. Instead, adopting a habit of making smaller tweaks and continual adjustments regularly (even daily) over an extended period of time can really make the difference. If you deal with post-war issues, you likely didn't develop them in a day and probably won't get rid of them in a day. But you can get rid of them over time if you play your cards right. Realizing this and doing something about it will help you redirect your line of fire so that you and your family are fighting together against the real enemy, instead of fighting with each other. Again, I understand. Things are not the same as they used to be and they never will be. They can be better than they used to be.

CHAPTER 10

DON'T SHOOT
YOURSELF IN THE FOOT

BRIAN

Credibility is a huge issue to me. I can usually tell when I'm listening to a guy who is making up war stories that never actually happened. I don't know why I have this ability, I just do. I think a lot of us who have actually been in combat have this sense about us. I guess I just have a very sensitive BS meter that picks up on stuff that just doesn't seem entirely right, courtesy of the U.S. military. I've even come across guys who claimed to have been awarded many of the same military decorations that I have been awarded and that some of my friends who never made it home were awarded. Come to find out oftentimes these individuals were never awarded any of these medals, and in some cases, hadn't ever actually deployed to a combat zone! There are a lot of people out there who are guilty of "Stolen Valor." But most of us who have actually been in combat and have lived through war can usually tell when something in a person's story doesn't entirely line up straight- especially if their story changes and becomes more and more extraordinary over time. Unfortunately, the freedom of speech we service members and veterans have fought and bled and died to defend now protects these types of pathetic and low- life individuals (and that's putting it nicely) who spit on the graves of America's fallen heroes, many of whom were good personal friends of mine and yours, in a shady attempt to glorify themselves.

I was sitting in a circle with about thirty other combat-wounded service members at one of the most pristine country club resorts in all the hill country of South Texas. Some of these men and women had been blown up like me; others had been shot, and some of them both! In fact, there was even a woman in attendance who was my mother's age and had FOUR Purple Hearts! Then there were others who had watched their friends die on the battlefields of Iraq and Afghanistan. On this particular occasion, I had been contracted by an organization to come and speak to these service members, veterans and their families. In addition to my regular talk, I was to lead numerous breakout sessions throughout the weekend addressing several topics of relevance pertaining to these service members and their families. My job wasn't to sit there, listen to a question, and merely regurgitate my own advice. My job was to get the ball rolling. My job wasn't to give them all the answers (which nobody truly has anyway), but to get them talking amongst themselves in order to assist them in finding their own solutions and coming to their own conclusions concerning the problems and issues they and their families were facing.

At one point a man in our circle spoke up in an angry, yet dignified tone,

"I'm sick and tired of talking to all of these doctors who have only read about these issues in a text book and have never been in combat themselves. They haven't been there.

They don't know what it's like. They can't help me because they've never been in my shoes!"

While I agree with the man's statement entirely, and even felt that same way myself after I returned home from the war in Afghanistan, I have to admit that there is a missing element to his case. Though this particular mentality is a very common one among many troops returning home from war, service members and veterans need to be open to all of their options if they are to find any sort of helpful advice in their journey to recovery.

In response to the man's frustration, I related his personal story and argument to the lives of some of the world's greatest and most talented athletes. First, in an effort not to burn my own credibility with him, I openly admitted to him that he was absolutely right about everything he had just said and I told him that I had felt that same way myself at one time. As he shook his head, somewhat smiling and acknowledging the fact that he was *"right,"* I quickly followed up my previous statement with a big *"BUT..."* (and this caught everybody's undivided attention, all eyes were now focused on me, intent and awaiting my next carefully chosen statement). I proceeded to ask him if he thought that Michael Jordan, indisputably one of the greatest basketball players to ever play the game, had ever worked with a coach—in season or out of season. He agreed that Michael Jordan did, indeed, likely work with a coach over the course of his career. I then asked him the same question about Tiger Woods, undoubtedly one of the greatest golfers in the world. He also agreed that Tiger Woods definitely worked with a coach, or several, over the course of his career. I then asked him another question,

"Who in the world do those coaches think they are, trying to show Michael Jordan how to play better basketball or Tiger Woods how to be a better golfer? After all, these guys are among the best in their sports and they are without question better at those sports than the guys coaching them. Why would these world-class athletes be willing to take advice from those who were much less talented or skilled in their respective sports than they were?"

You could have heard a pin drop in the room. After a brief pause and a moment of silence to contemplate the question, I began addressing my take on the answer. Despite their obvious and superior skill in their sports of choice, both of these world-class athletes apparently realized that there can be great value in an objective and outside perspective, even from an individual who is less talented in their sport of choice. The view is very different for a wide receiver on a football field simply trying not to get killed by a blood-thirsty linebacker than it is for someone who is sitting up in the stands watching the game from a distance. The person sitting in the stands has a broader, more objective view of the game than the player who is actually on the field and does all he can according to his own present tunnel vision. The person up in the stands doesn't know what it's like to be the player on the field, but can still offer an outside, and often beneficial, perspective for the player. What does the basketball player do if he is doing most of his techniques the right way, yet keeps sticking his elbows out while trying to shoot free-throws and continually misses the shot? A coach who is observing from the outside can often identify small errors in the player's methods that the player can't necessarily see on their own because they are the one "in the game" and, consequently, the coach can help the player slightly tweak his or her techniques and habits, even if by only a millimeter, in order to better perfect his or her performance and become even better at the sport. You may be only one degree off, from where you are trying to go in life, but over a great distance or an extended period of time that one degree off can land you in a completely different destination than you originally intended.

When it comes to doctors working with military service members and veterans it is often no different. These medical professionals can likely offer you food for thought that can help lead you, or at the least spur thoughts in your mind that can help lead you, in the right direction. Most of them, obviously, have no clue what it's like to be in combat and haven't experienced the atrocities of war first hand as many of us have and we are accurate in pointing out that fact. But at the same time we must not remain ignorant to the fact, and so self-indulged, that though these individuals have never experienced war themselves as many of us have, that others, including doctors can offer us a unique and alternate perspective that can allow us to tweak our own ways and methods in order to become better in several areas of our lives. I'll be the first to admit that there are some really bad doctors out there who simply don't care about anybody but themselves, and honestly don't seem to have any idea what they are doing. However, in my experience, most of them have proper motives and sincerely care about people. I will always give most of them the benefit of the doubt and, when I do, I'm usually right.

At the end of the day, the doctor will go home to his or her family and you will go home to yours. Whether or not you choose to be open to alternate and outside perspectives that can make you a better person is entirely up to you as an individual and has no bearing on the quality of life of those trying to help you. Becoming better and moving beyond certain life circumstances is a personal choice you will eventually have to make. If you choose simply not to make a choice, you have already done so and the benefits or consequences will be yours and only yours.

CHAD

Knowing Brian personally, I can say this is a topic he is very passionate about. And I can also say that from my personal experience and experience with others, the authenticity of your experience is fundamental in recovery.

When you look at an iceberg, you only see ten percent of it; you miss the ninety percent below the surface. I feel that people are that way, too. If we could just be authentic and transparent, others could understand us so much better.

Sometimes I have to ask myself, if everyone was Special Forces, then who was fighting on the front lines, and where the heck was all the essential support? Why is it that everyone has to claim to be Special Operations or "worked with them?" Yes, I spent my entire military time in Special Operations...no, I really did! However, I have always had the highest level of respect for the true courage and grit of the infantryman who charges towards gunfire and will fight to the death for ten feet of ground in order to move our nation ten feet closer to victory. At times I've stood in sheer admiration of the self-sacrifice of the field physician who could be in the civilian world making tons of cash but chooses to serve instead. Or the service mechanic who can fix any piece of military equipment in the most adverse conditions and under the pressure of critical time restraints and hostility. I love my military brothers and can't fathom why they can't just be proud of the great services they do.

With that, I'd have to say my biggest pet peeve, and an area I have little patience for, is faking symptoms of PTSD. I have a great deal of patience, but I have to say this tests me to the max, and I have a knack for spotting it a mile away. My "fakedar" alerts and next thing you know I'm hearing stories about nightmares, flashbacks, and rage, but the stories are always over the top. I can't tell you how many times I've heard, *"There I was, my .45 in one hand and a bottle of Jack Daniels in the other, not sure what shot I was going to take next!" And when I hear the words, "That was my first confirmed kill,"* I almost puke in mouth.

My friends at Ranger Up make some really cool Military Videos. They made one a few months ago about PTSD and Combat Vet Fakers called, "Ranger Up - Stolen Valor." It is actually hilarious—true, but sad! These jokers ruin it for every real warrior who really needs help. In my opinion, anyone faking symptoms does have a problem—it's just not PTSD. And they do need help—just not from veterans' programs.

There was a great tragedy last year when a guy was exposed as a fake. In addition to being the poster boy of a national PTSD organization, he was the head counselor. He was actually a phenomenal guy, and great at working with other veterans. Unfortunately, the depth of his lies and the damage he caused to his organization and the veterans he had helped were so devastating that he will never counsel veterans again.

The guy had served, but only in a support role for ten years, and had never been overseas. Apparently he had gone to medical to be seen for anxiety, and was basically told to get over it because there were guys coming home from Iraq and Afghanistan who had real problems. That led him to go to another doctor and claim to be Army Special Forces, Delta

Force, with combat action in multiple countries around the world. He claimed several Purple Hearts, Bronze Stars, and even a Silver Star—all for valor. The story grew so big and other people were proud to work with this Spec Ops Hero. Soon he was put in the spotlight. He even tried to validate his story by crafting a fake DD-214 and getting a Silver Star license plate. He even had me and his own family fooled. I'm sure stories like this make most vets angry as a wet cat—but at the end of the day, you have a guy who wanted help, needed help, and somehow felt that lying about his experience and his symptoms would be a solution. It wasn't.

I spoke with this man after he was exposed. He said that during the years of living this lie, his one hope and prayer was to be exposed one day so that he could finally get help for his anxiety problem. He was his own obstacle, and became an obstacle to many others.

As you can see—and many of you may have seen firsthand—there are a lot of real, fake, and scenarios in between, but simply elaborating on your war story seems to be the most common of all. It's far too common. In my experience, a couple of things commonly happen with veterans in this situation. One, they cannot understand why they have such a hard time with the symptoms of PTSD, so they think if they embellish on their experience they can justify the anger, depression, and other symptoms that generally affect everyone around them. Then, the lie or facade they build around them becomes one of their biggest obstacles to healing.

I rarely ever talk about the details of my experiences in Afghanistan, for a couple of reasons. For one, my experiences weren't meant for others or the general public; and two, they just really don't matter in my healing. The true story I need to talk about is what happened when I got home, how I have dealt with it, what damage was caused, and how can I productively move forward. I recently had a Marine come through our program who turned out to be a true hero. He was CI HET (Counter Intelligence Human Exploitation Teams). This young warrior had been through hell—lost lots of team mates, did things he carried tremendous guilt over, and suffers from a severe TBI (Traumatic Brain Injury). Prior to his arrival at our Fight Club program at Eagles Summit Ranch, this Marine had been through every program in the book and nothing had worked. His beautiful family was taking the brunt of it and his wife and children were desperate for a glimpse of hope.

I had a limited amount of time to discover why he wasn't getting better. It was clear he was blocking out all help because he had decided that his experience was too "secret" to talk about. Therefore, he had classified himself as hopeless and had given up. As a Marine, it drives me up the wall to see another Marine quit. I planned my strategy and waited. I waited for him to pull that garbage secret squirrel line in front of the class. Then I intentionally called him out in front of the other warriors, and in a pointed proclamation I told him what he had needed to hear for a very long time:

"No one gives a crap about your war experience. Everyone in here has one, and we are here to talk about what you are going to do about it."

The room went quiet, and his jaw hit the floor, but he knew I was right. From that point on, he fully engaged in the program and the changes were immediately evident. We smashed down a wall he had built based on either embellishing or overdramatizing his own experience and allowing it to be an obstacle in his healing. A few days after he went home, we got a message from his wife who was in shock as to what we had done to him. The path to healing had finally begun.

While that method of counseling worked for me, could you imagine if some clinical psychologist had told this Marine, "No one gives a crap about your war experience!" Man, someone dial 911 because Doc is about to get thrown through the window! You see, there are things I can say and other combat vets can say to our struggling peers, and it's necessary. These guys can look in my eyes and know that I know where they have been and what they are struggling with. And that is a necessary part of healing, to lock arms with your brothers and work through moving forward.

However, like Brian, I agree we can gain a lot from others who have not been in combat. As a professional fighter, more often than not, I have been coached by subject matter experts who I would crush in the cage if I were to compete against them. Most of these coaches have never even been in the cage, but I trust them. Why? Because without their coaching, I wouldn't have the tools and skills to win. It is combined teamwork between my skills and abilities and their expertise that seals the victory. I love that God made us with such a lack of independent ability. Even the greatest athlete in the world is worthless without coaches and team mates. Because of this, I never look at fighting as an individual sport. I think it is one of the greatest team sports in the world, and feel so privileged to have stepped in that cage so many times to represent my team the coaches, training partners, and supporters that give me the ability to be there. We win together.

However, like that CI Marine I mentioned earlier, I did the exact same thing for a time. I wouldn't talk to anyone for some of the same reasons. I felt I didn't fit in with anyone in this civilian world. If you weren't a gun-slinger, I didn't want to talk to you. Not many true gun-slingers in suburban America, so it made for a lonely life for a while.

At what we thought was the very end of our marriage, my wife made a final attempt to find me help. She called our church and no pastors were available. A man named Steve Toth called back and spoke with her. Steve was never in the military. He was a New Yorker, a career business man, and now a Texas State Legislator. Steve and Kathy thought they had the perfect solution. He knew a pastor who was a combat vet and retired

Navy SEAL; his son was a SEAL, and he was a man's man. I was sure to love this guy and he could help me. I met Steve and was introduced to this Super Pastor Navy SEAL dude, who was great by the way…but in the end I fell in love with the heart of Steve Toth and he became the mentor I needed to teach me how to drop my guard so I could begin to heal. Who would have thought? Not me. But I love this man and he saved my life.

It would be eighteen months of mentorship by Steve before I would align myself with other veterans like Dave Roever. The work Steve had started would be carried on by my fellow veterans, but it all started with someone who never served in the military. Steve is the furthest thing from a "gun slinger" I could imagine, but he has my respect and admiration, and my gratitude forever for saving my marriage and my life.

CHAPTER 11

SUICIDE – A FINAL SOLUTION?

BRIAN

He was blown up *fifteen times* while fighting in the war on terror. Fifteen different times while inside fifteen different vehicles (and people think my story of getting blown up twice is bad!). He miraculously walked away unscathed from the first fourteen explosions, but the last one severely injured him and killed everybody else in his vehicle. His wife and kids back home had no idea what he was dealing with. After returning home from deployment, severely injured, confused, and overwhelmed with survivor's guilt, he put a loaded gun in his mouth and pulled the trigger.

Two weeks later, I sat across from him in a conference room listening to him tell bits and pieces of his story for the very first time. It was a humbling experience to know that just two weeks prior, while I was visiting with my family and enjoying the greater things in life, this man who is a husband and father was trying to kill himself. But for some strange, "unknown" reason, nothing happened when he pulled the trigger that day. The weapon misfired! There was no question as to whether or not the gun was loaded and had a round in the chamber. It did because that was how he always carried it. He knew no other way.

After sharing his story, he looked across the table at me and said:

"You know, Brian… I think there might be a reason I'm still here."

I strongly agreed with him.

After returning home to his wife and kids at the end of the week after the program ended, he decided to start a business! You may be wondering what happened that week that caused such a fast and unexpected turn around for the better in this guy's life. Something happens when you get around other people who have similar experiences to your own and are moving forward productively in life. The silent implications that need no words, "We've all been there, too. We can relate. We know what it's like. But now it's time to move on and we will help you, but we aren't going to cut you any slack. It's for your own good and you'll thank us someday." Sometimes the best advice for a person comes from someone just like them. For combat veterans who may be struggling, the tough, yet concerned, words of another combat veteran can be highly effective. These are words that can sometimes only be safely spoken by someone else who has been to war. There are some bits of advice and words that I've earned the right to say to other combat veterans that if said by a civilian would shoot down their credibility and probably land them in the hospital. Sometimes we have to earn the right to speak into somebody else's life.

Another gripping story always comes to mind when I think on the topic of suicide. It's the story of a young girl, in her early twenties, who served as a Combat Medic fighting the war in Iraq. While riding through one of Iraq's major cities, one of the vehicles in her convoy hit a roadside bomb and exploded. Given that her vehicle wasn't the one to hit the bomb, she was fine. She quickly responded and made her way to the blasted vehicle, which was up in flames at that point. Inside the vehicle sat one of her best friends. She grabbed the door handle and attempted to open her friend's door in order to help the other soldier to safety. But when she did, the door would not open. Frantically, she pounded and pulled on the door but with no success. It was her against the door; the door made of armor plating and bulletproof glass for windows, a door that was created to be impenetrable by design. That day this young and valiant soldier watched her friend burn to death through three inches of bulletproof glass. Her experience is obviously an unimaginable one. Her sense of survivor's guilt, combined with her inability to stop the horrifying memories from involuntarily replaying in her mind, drove her to several suicide attempts.

"I can't get the images out of my head," she would say.

Suicide has become an epidemic in our world, especially among the ranks of our military and veteran communities. Does it make sense that after fighting valiantly, serving honorably, and surviving life in a war zone and then returning home, some choose to kill themselves? There have been times when it seemed as if we were losing more service members and veterans to suicide due to unresolved post-war issues than we did in actual combat casualties. Unfortunately, throughout the history of 21st century wars, this has been true in many cases.

How do we get through to somebody who has decided they are at their rope's end and life is no longer worth living?

THE ANSWER: Give them hope. Give it to them in any way, shape, or form. In any manner in which they'll take it or accept it, give it to them because hope is the greatest enemy of suicide. It only takes a small spark to start a wildfire and it only takes one small glimmer of hope to keep a person from making a drastic and life-altering decision that will negatively send a tragic and dramatic ripple effect throughout the world around them and the generations that follow.

People kill themselves every day because they lose hope. They don't believe life will ever get better. They think that because life is rough in the present moment that it will never change. They don't believe they will ever escape whatever it is that is driving them to that point of unbearable misery. The contributing factors seem almost endless. But what many of them fail to realize is that the suffering they're experiencing in the present moment pales in comparison to future they have to look forward to if they will simply choose to hang on and continue moving forward in life. It may not be a "normal" life as they once knew it, but it is possible to live an incredible life in spite of bad experiences. It is possible to move forward and live a satisfying and fulfilling life in the "new normal." To do so, each person has to recover or find what makes them feel alive, and then begin pushing the buttons and pulling the triggers on those devices in their lives that will allow them to "reactivate" those devices.

After I was blown up and horribly injured by the suicide bomber in Afghanistan, I never became suicidal. I don't know why. I just didn't and I'm glad. Everybody has their demons and suicide simply wasn't one of mine. Though I never dealt with suicide, there did come a point where I didn't care if I lived or not because the constant pain I was experiencing at the time seemed to be never-ending. But I found something to do with it all. I found an outlet I was able to plug in to and begin releasing a lot of that steadily increasing pressure that we often find building up in our lives. My outlet ended up turning into somewhat of a career. Who knew? It has led me to where I am today as an author and speaker who has the unique privilege of traveling the globe, creating products and programs that help other people become more productive, and living a life I could have never imagined and I wouldn't trade it for anything. I'm even to the point that I can honestly say I am glad everything happened to me as it did in Afghanistan. This may not be the case for everybody and I understand that. But what I experienced in war has made me a better, wiser, more intelligent and experienced person who now has the insight and ability to do something only made possible by such an experience.

There is a light at the end of the tunnel and it is not a freight train. Chad and I are both very strong believers in purpose. That is, that there is a greater and overarching purpose for our lives and yours. There is a purpose for the experiences you've had and for the experiences we've had and that belief has been one of the strongest driving forces for the success we've both been able to enjoy and see come about in our lives. We've seen great success not only in our careers, but also in our families, and in many other areas of our lives. Personally, I believe that my purpose in life is to help you find yours.

I don't know if you believe in the idea of destiny (as cheesy as that term may sound to some, but bear with me) or the idea of there being an ultimate purpose for your life. Whether or not you believe in God, destiny, or a higher being of some sort is entirely up to you. But having a solid and unshakable sense of definite purpose will certainly help a person through the tough times if they believe and live according to the belief that, perhaps, everything happens for a reason and that a greater good is going to come from their situation. It was this same belief that gave me the drive I needed to keep moving forward when I was laying in a hospital bed burned second and third degree after the suicide attack. When I was suffering intense physical pain and didn't know when it would ever end, it was this belief alone that provided the internal fuel I needed to not give up and begin making sense of it all. Never dismiss the possibilities you aren't able to yet see. Regardless, it is critical to realize the difference between history (the past) and destiny (the future). Though the past can have influence on the future, we have the ability to choose whether or not that influence will be good or bad. Your past is not your future, though your past can prove to be a very valuable asset to your future. Your history is not your destiny (destination). Don't believe me? If you're driving down the interstate doing 70 mph and only looking backwards in your rear-view mirror, you WILL crash and burn. You will only be able to go so far before going completely off the road and into a tree or building. It can only end badly. It's alright, even necessary at times, to glance backwards temporarily and learn from our experiences, but we can't keep our eyes fixed there. When you look back, look back with the intention of pulling lessons out of your past and then apply those lessons to what you see ahead in order to have a better future. Don't drown in your experience, use it. Your past experiences can be a burden or a school. You can learn from them or you can die from them.

Your history, your past experiences, whether good or bad, can either poison you or propel you. It all has to do with what you choose to do with them. If you keep wondering "why" something happened, choose to put that idea to the side for now and instead begin focusing on "what" you can do with your past experiences. This tiny shift in thinking will ultimately take you down an entirely different path in life, a path that for me has been more than worth going down. This was one of the major choices I made that changed everything for me after my own life-altering war injury.

A Two-Sided Coin

The common debate concerning suicide is a two-sided coin. Let me explain… With just about every group I speak to and every breakout session I lead for military or veterans organizations as a resiliency trainer I hear the same two sides concerning the matter of suicide debated.

Suicide, as with any topic concerning the right to life or death, is a controversial one depending on who you ask. But again, in my experience there are two primary sides to this issue that I usually end up facing in a discussion group.

First, I hear the side of those who critically and actively oppose it. These individuals are typically not the ones contemplating or attempting suicide, but others who are simply voicing their opinion on the matter. More often than not, I hear them make the following statement: *"Suicide is the most selfish decision a person could ever make."*
I can't say I disagree with that statement.

But then, I hear the pleas and thought processes of those who are contemplating or have attempted suicide. Their perspective seems equally valid, but is very different. I often hear them say things like:"Nobody knows what it's like to be me. Nobody knows what I go through. They've never been through what I've been through. They don't know how heavy this pain is that I have to live with every day. It isn't going away. I can't carry it any longer. People tell me suicide is selfish, but is it not just as selfish, or even cruel and inhumane, to make a person who is in so much pain continue existing in that agony and misery? It is cruel to make me have to go on living in it."Again, I can't say I entirely disagree with this person's statement either.

However, suicide is a very self-"ish" event, in that it focuses inwardly on only the suicidal person themselves with no regard to those whose lives will be shattered by it: family, kids, friends, and loved ones.

If we are to help those who are suicidal, we must not only give them hope, but must also get them thinking about other people. We must help them shift their focus from only themselves and help them get their focus and attention onto those they love and care about most. As many of us know, suicide doesn't merely hurt the person who commits the act. Rather, it devastates, and often destroys, the lives of friends, children, family members, and loved ones of the person who decides to kill themselves.

Not too long ago my friend Matt brought to my attention a shocking, but eye-opening, study concerning suicide. According to a thirty-year study conducted by Johns Hopkins University, children whose parents commit suicide are three times more likely to commit suicide themselves than other children who have living parents. Additionally, these same children who have parents who committed suicide are twice as likely to end up institutionalized for depression and other psychiatric disorders than other children who have living parents. (Dr. Holly C. Wilcox, 2010)

Given this one study alone, is suicide a selfish act? In spite of a person's desire to justify the act and given the obvious and possibly destructive effect on the lives of others, the answer is an obvious yes.

Next time you talk to someone who is contemplating suicide, ask them if they love their children. Then, let them know how likely their children are to end up like they have if they choose to continue and go through with it. If, in light of these thoughts and statistics a person chooses to commit suicide anyway, how else could anybody define the situation except as a selfish one? If somebody is willing to leave their child all alone in this world, knowing full well that their kid is much more likely to kill themselves as well or end up institutionalized if they choose to follow through with their decision to commit suicide, then "selfish" is the only term anybody could ever give to them.

I sympathize with anybody who ever has, or is, contemplating suicide. I can't pretend to know what they've been through and I never would. I can't say I personally know what it's like to be suicidal because I never have been. But as I previously mentioned, I do know what it's like to not want to live anymore. I know what it's like to be in so much pain that being unconscious or dead seems to be the only logical escape. The greatest example of this came in my own life after I was attacked by the suicide bomber in Kandahar. I was burned 2nd and 3rd degree on both of my hands, my face, and my neck. When I arrived at Brooke Army Medical Center in San Antonio, Texas, the nurses pulled out razor blades and began shaving and tearing and ripping the dead, dirty, burned, charred flesh from my body while I was still awake and completely conscious. Like tearing the skin off of a piece of burnt chicken, my skin slid right off of my body. No words can describe how painful that experience was and in that moment (or should I say that "20- 30 minute period of pure hell") I prayed to die. I wasn't about to make it happen myself, I've never dealt with suicide, but I sure prayed hard that it would just happen to me on its own so I would finally be free from the pain once and for all. But my prayers were not answered that night. Today I thank God for unanswered prayers. I didn't quite understand in that moment the entirety of what I was asking for, but now I do, and I'm glad I didn't get what I was asking for. Though I wouldn't wish the pain I endured upon anybody, I am a better, wiser, and more successful person today because of having gone through that experience. I am better now, having gone through the fire, than I was when I originally went in.

I was blessed with the gift of almost dying at the young age of twenty-one years old (courtesy of the suicide bomber in Kandahar, Afghanistan). But I can now see how incredibly fortunate I am to have such a unique and uncommon perspective on life that can only come through such an experience. I won't lie when I say that I now live a totally awesome life and I don't apologize for it. The best things in my life were born out of the worst. I've never lived a better life since almost losing it.

As I mentioned previously, our history is not our future. Our history has the ability to poison us or propel us. It all depends on how we choose to use it (or not use it). I believe there is a greater purpose for me still being alive today and that there is a greater purpose for you as well. Given my own life experiences, it is difficult for me to see it any other way.

If you're like me, you've lost friends who died in combat. They didn't come back home to their families as you and I did. The best way we can honor them, the price they paid, their memory and the lives they lived, is to do something productive with the lives we still have. If you're struggling with your own issues then start searching for a way to get over them and move past them. If you don't find any solutions immediately, then keep searching. I have no sympathy for a person who will simply lie down and die and stop moving forward in life without first exhausting every possible resource. The cold-blooded truth of the matter is this: If you had friends who were killed in action as I did, those friends are gone and there isn't anything we can do about it. My friend and roommate Sgt. Cody Legg is gone and, as painful as it is to admit, he is never coming back. The fastest and easiest way to spit on the graves of your friends and loved ones who didn't make it home is to give up and waste the life that you still have. I still have a choice to do something with my life, but my friend Cody doesn't because that was taken from him when he attempted to drag two of his wounded buddies out of the kill zone during an ambush. He willingly gave up everything, every tiny fabric of life that made up his existence- his family members, his girlfriend and any future they would've had together, his money and possessions, friends back home, future dreams and goals, the finer things in life that he enjoyed most. He put it all on the line and ended up losing it so that his buddies who had been gunned down and were lying helpless and exposed to enemy gunfire might survive and be able to live another day. Every day that we choose to hang on a little bit longer, live better lives and continue moving forward, we honor our friends and loved ones who no longer have that choice.

If you are contemplating suicide, remember that life is not about you. It is about others. And when you choose to take your focus off of yourself and put it onto others, it is amazing how incredibly quick you will begin developing an internal sense of purpose and lacking a desire to simply die. Doing this won't always take away all of the issues or the pain you may be struggling with, but it will cause those issues to become purpose-driven and purpose is what we all, ultimately, are searching for. Be willing to rob the grave that was dug for you. Again, a sense of purpose gives a person hope and hope is the greatest enemy of suicide.

CHAD

Twenty-two a day! I do a lot of public speaking and everyone seems so shocked when I say we lose twenty-two of our veterans a day to suicide, which is almost one every hour. Twenty-two a day, 8,030 a year according a study conducted by the VA (Department of Veteran Affairs, 2013). Think about it... Wow!! That's unacceptable. In Vietnam there were nearly

60,000 American deaths, but the number we don't hear is that there were 160,000 Vietnam veteran suicides. Almost three times the number of veterans died at their own hands than at the hands of the enemy.

Stopping suicides and saving families is my biggest motivation for doing what I do in working with other veterans because the two are so close to home for me. In addition to almost losing my family, it shames me to admit it, but I faced the thought of suicide myself—not to end my pain but the pain I felt I was dragging my family through...the shame I felt for becoming someone I wasn't. Two things kept me from doing it. One was the fact that I believe we are all eternal, immortal beings created by God for eternity either with Him or without Him...so a fear of hell may have been my saving grace. The second reason is my family. I couldn't imagine how my sons who follow everything I do would react. Later, I would learn that one out of three children of a suicide parent follow in suicide. As a man with three children, that not so fun fact broke my heart and brought me to tears.

There is always a brighter day and I am sure glad to be alive! I know God had a plan for my life and I'm happy to be living it, and I think the people I'm closest to in this world are glad to have me here too.

Even knowing the statistics and stories as well as I do, it never ceases to amaze me how many warriors come to our programs who have had failed suicide attempts. I don't mean the fake attempts and cries for attention- *I'm talking a bottle of*

Ambien, a bottle of Percocet, and a bottle of vodka, then laying down and going to sleep. Miraculously, somehow someone has an intuition to pay a late night visit and find them. As Brian mentioned earlier in the book, another soldier had his pistol misfire in his mouth just two weeks before arriving at our program because he didn't feel he could handle life anymore. After the misfire, he figured it wasn't time to go and he'd give our ranch a chance. In both cases, these men are doing great now, and love being alive. I couldn't imagine these men not being alive today due to simply caving into one low moment of weakness and being successful at finishing a job that the enemy in Iraq or Afghanistan couldn't.

If the self-destruction of your own eternity isn't bad enough, the devastation to others you leave behind is life-long. There is a female speaker Brian and I work with at Eagles Summit Ranch. Her son is Army, 10th Special Forces Group. She is an amazing lady of strength with a heart of gold for the warriors, but she has had tragedy strike her family more than once. She lost her youngest son to a drunk driver, and then a short time later her husband committed suicide. She tells the story of not only the pain and sense of abandonment, but the anger towards him. She was so angry and hurt that she removed every trace of his existence from the home… every piece of clothing, every picture, anything that he could be remembered by.

I think of that and my legacy. I want my life to mean something. I want to leave a legacy. My life and military service has value and meaning, and so does yours! And maybe today or maybe years from now, you will not have shame or guilt, but pride in your service. You can have a legacy, a great one, a name to be remembered. Don't end it with an exclamation point of failure, and don't leave a wake of destruction for others. There is always a brighter day, but there is darkness before the light.

In a speech he made before the war in Iraq began, Saddam Hussein was quoted as saying: *"The Mongols of our age will commit suicide at the gates of Baghdad."* Though he was wrong, unfortunately he wasn't far off—just look at the numbers. Every combat veteran should hang on and fight through their personal battles—if for no other reason than to prove a murderous dictator wrong. This lunatic of a man is now dead and we must not allow him or our other enemies to claim and win the war over us and our families, even in death. To allow this to happen is to willingly surrender and hand our enemies the final victory. We will never surrender. We will continue to fight and we will continue to win!

AFTER ACTION REVIEW

After deploying to war and fighting the battles you've fought, it is no secret that you will be REDEPLOYED to another war upon returning home, a war of a different nature with a new battleground and terrain, new enemies with new tactics, and it will require you to constantly fight, adapt to, and overcome each of them—which is exactly what you've been trained and equipped to do since day one when you joined the military.

There will always be another tough battle to fight. That's life, so get used to it. You must continually be willing to fight and win at all costs and never surrender. The military didn't necessarily equip you to fight and win the war at home when you joined and that is the reason we decided to write this book: to begin equipping and educating you to win the greater war that is taking place whether you like it or not. This greater war is not for control over a piece of land, however. This war is for your peace of mind, your quality of life, the lives of your spouse and children, those you care about, and your very way of life. Visualize the win and claim your victory.

Everybody has bad experiences and you are no exception. The difference is made in what you choose to do with those experiences. The battles you face or may face in the future are common among those like you, including us!

In the military we are always given a mission. But after returning home from war, being released from active duty, and returning to civilian life most of us lose that sense of mission and purpose – at least to some extent or another. Each of us has to begin finding a new mission in life after the military. The guys who get out and find a new mission in life after coming home from war are hard to miss. Unfortunately, so are the guys who didn't find a new mission. In life we must always have a mission and it must continue. Search out and find a new mission as if your life depended on it because it does.

As combat veterans and the authors of this book, we know what war is like. We've both been there, lived it, and are now productively living in its aftermath. We will never leave a fallen comrade. Continue the fight with us and fight alongside us in this war as you REDEPLOY.

Afterword By
Greg Drobny

Not that long ago, the public voice available on behalf of the veteran community was relatively small and, to be quite honest, fairly unassuming and unaggressive. In recent years, that has thankfully begun to change.

Being a writer for the Ranger Up and Rhino Den community has given me several great opportunities, but none more near and dear to my heart than the concept of providing a public voice to those who don't have one and thereby shining some light on certain issues such as the ones covered in this book. I can confidently speak for the others at Ranger Up and The Rhino Den when I say that veterans who have returned from combat and are suffering—either mentally or physically or both—are at the top of our lists of things that need to be addressed and have brought to the attention of more and more people.

REDEPLOYED is a book that not only addresses the important issues faced by returning combat veterans, but it smashes the misperceptions people may have about the problem while laying out a road map of how to deal with them—all from people who know what they are talking about, both from an experience point of view as well as an educational one. Chad and Brian are not short on experience, to be sure. But what sets them apart more than their

background is their willingness to lay open their own wounds for all to see; being honest in their own struggles and how they faced them makes this a truly unique and needed work.

I was introduced via email to Chad Robichaux by another veteran and Ranger Up alumnus, retired LTC Kelly Crigger. Prior to that introduction, I was unaware of who Chad and Brian— and the Mighty Oaks Program they are a part of—were and what they were doing. From the moment I started looking into their organization, however, I have been continually impressed and more and more grateful for their continued dedication to the veteran community. It is truly inspiring to know that men like this exist and are out there, every day, working their tails off to address problems that have been largely swept under the rug by large bureaucracies. We live in a time with a federal government that has exploded in size and, as a result, numerous categories within that system have been either minimized or simply forgotten.

At Ranger up and The Rhino Den, we speak frequently of the ".45%"—the very small percentage of the population of the United States who served in the military. We understand that there is a difference between that .45% and the rest of the country, and an even more pronounced difference between those who have seen the horrors of war and those who greet them when they return home. Chad and Brian have, with this book, gone far beyond addressing those differences; they have shown why they exist and how to manage them.

It is in that regard that this book is for a much wider audience

than just returning combat veterans. Those who are in the family of a combat veteran or those who work in the field of veteran's advocacy would benefit highly from what is written in these pages. Point of fact, there are a disproportionate number of "psychologists" employed by the Veterans Administration who *should have this be required reading prior to treating any more patients.* I highly encourage anyone who is even remotely connected to the veteran community to take a few hours of your time to become acquainted with REDEPLOYED.

Isaiah 6:8 is a familiar Bible verse to the warrior community. "Then I heard the voice of the Lord saying, 'Whom shall I send? And who will go for us?' And I said, 'Here am I. Send me.'" REDEPLOYED is a book for those who answered the call of their country by saying "send me." It is for those who said those words and realized that life would never be the same, for better or worse, because of the path that call took them on.

From those at Ranger Up and The Rhino Den, let me just say that our own dedication to those who answered the call and chose to serve is only inspired and made better by the work of men like Chad and Brian. REDEPLOYED will be on our recommended reading list for a long time to come.

A MUST-READ for returning combat veterans and their families!
—**Greg "Mr. Twisted" Drobny**
Ranger Up and Rhino Den Writer

ABOUT THE AUTHORS

Brian C. Fleming

US Army Infantry
International Author and Speaker
Veteran Advocate and PTSD Strategist

"Fleming is a combat-wounded veteran, international author and speaker. He now serves as one of America's Top Resiliency Trainers for the U.S. Military and is a leading authority on effectively battling Post-Traumatic Stress.

He served as a Team Leader in an Infantry Platoon with the U.S. Army's 10th Mountain Division. A Purple Heart recipient, Fleming's vehicle was blown up twice and he sustained multiple life-threatening injuries from the attack of a suicide bomber who exploded three-feet away from him in Kandahar, Afghanistan on July 24th, 2006. He awoke, burned and bloody, laying face-down in a ditch on the side of the road. He sustained 2nd and 3rd degree burns to both of his hands, his face, and his neck. After enduring reconstructive surgery and fourteen months of burn treatment and rehabilitation at Brooke Army Medical Center in San Antonio, Texas, he was medically discharged from the Army. His book, Never the Same, was later published about his war experiences in Afghanistan.

A popular speaker among corporations, associations, and colleges, he also speaks and conducts resiliency training on military bases and for military and veteran's organizations globally, teaching them how to be more resilient on the job and at home, and how to stand firm when everything around them is blowing up.

Fleming has personally mentored over 1,000 combat veterans from the War on Terror in the areas of business, marriage and family, faith, life skills, and how to effectively battle Post-Traumatic Stress.

Appearing on Fox News, CNN, CSPAN, ESPN, CBS, and ABC, as well as being featured in USA Today, Fleming is a frequently sought after guest of the news media concerning military and veteran's issues and has shared the stage with several other leaders of influence, including the President of the United States.

Brian and his wife Jamie have two children, Blake and Kailey, and live in Dallas, Texas."

Military Officials, Commanders, and Chaplains, go to:

www.MilitarySpeakerTrainer.com

All others- For media and speaking inquiries or booking Brian Fleming to make an appearance at your next event or on your program, contact us today at:

www.BrianCFleming.com

or Call: (719) 569-4321

www.Facebook.com/TheBlownUpGuy

www.Twitter.com/BrianCFleming

"Brian's presentation was an excellent choice for our annual Wingman Day! He told his story in a way that our Airmen could relate to and truly drove home the importance of making the right choices! His willingness to share his story will help many service members in the future."

—Jack D. Sweet, Community Support Coordinator, 55th Wing- Offutt Air Force Base, Nebraska

Chad M. Robichaux, BCPC, MBA

Founder & President of Mighty Oaks Foundation
USMC Force Recon Veteran
Best Selling Author
Pro MMA Champion

Chad M. Robichaux is the President and Founder of the Mighty Oaks Foundation, a leading military non-profit serving the US Military active duty and veteran communities with highly successful peer-to-peer faith based combat trauma programs and combat resiliency conferences. Chad and his team are dedicated to helping America's military warriors and their families suffering from the "unseen wounds" of combat such as Post Traumatic Stress Disorder (PTSD). Their effort is on the front line to intercede and end the climbing 22 per day veteran suicide rate and the tragic divorce epidemic in military families. To date the program has over 1,200 alumni and has reached tens of thousands active duty service members through resiliency conferences.

Chad is a former Special Operations Force Recon Marine and DoD Contractor with eight deployments to Afghanistan as part of a Joint Special Operations Command (JSOC) Task Force. He has earned an MBA and is a Board Certified Pastoral Counselor with a focus on PTSD. Chad and his wife, Kathy, have been married for 21 years, and have three children. After years of deployments their family personally faced the challenges of PTSD. They now share a story of a victory in Christ through the struggles our warriors face returning home and have dedicated their lives to sharing that story to mentor others like them. Chad is a widely sought after public speaker and subject matter expert on PTSD, military and veterans' issues providing advisory to the nation's highest ranking flag officers and advised the current presidential administration on the best and most-effective faith-based solutions for veteran's care. Chad has testified in Veteran Courts regarding combat trauma and PTSD, wrote a best-selling book on the subject and has been featured on such media outlets as Fox News, Forbes, The O'Reilly Factor, The Blaze with Glenn Beck, USA Today, Christian Post, Focus on The Family, The 700 Club, and a short biography film by I Am Second. In addition to Chad's military service he has served our nation as a Special Agent with the US Federal Air Marshal Service and the US State Department as a Surveillance Detection Senior Program Manager. Chad is also a Medal of Valor Recipient for his bravery beyond the call of duty in law enforcement.

Outside of his work with veterans Chad and his sons train and teaches Brazilian Jiu-Jitsu. He is a 3rd Degree Black Belt and a Former Pro MMA World Champion who has used his platform to advocate for civilian support of America's Warriors returning home while competing in the sports biggest events such as NBC's World Series of Fighting, Showtime's StrikeForce, MTV2's Bellator FC, and Legacy FC on HDNet & AXStv.

REFERENCES

VA,. (2013, February 1st). News. Retrieved
February 1, 2013, from US Dept. of Veteran
Affairs Mental Health Services Suicide Prevention
Program, Janet Kemp, RN, PhD, Robert Bossarte,
PhD- Department of Veterans Affairs:
http://www.va.gov/opa/docs/Suicide-Data-
Report-2012-final.pdf

Dr. Holly C. Wilcox, P. (2010, April 21). *Johns
Hopkins Childrens Center.* Retrieved January 1,
2013, from http://www.hopkinschildrens.org/
Children-Who-Lose-a-Parent-to-Suicide-More-
Likely-to-Die-the- Same-Way.aspx

Hemingway, E. (1936). *On The Blue Water: A
Gulf Stream Letter.* New York: Esquire Publishing
Company.

Scott, R. (Director). (2000). *Gladiator*
[Motion Picture].

Fincher, D. (Director). (1999). *Fight Club*
[Motion Picture].

FLEMING

Brian's first vehicle that was blown up (April 18th, 2006)

This is where Brian was seated when the vehicle exploded.

The second explosion: Brian's vehicle following the suicide attack in Kandahar. He was sitting in the front passenger seat. His door is blasted open in this picture.

The scarce remains of the suicide bomber's vehicle.

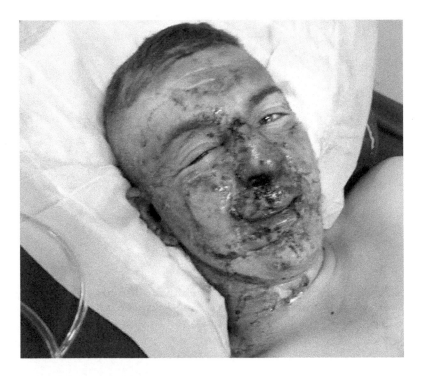

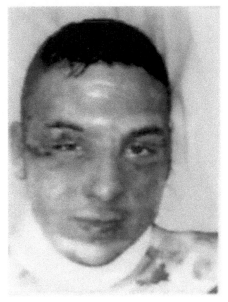

**Brian at Kandahar
Air Field immediately
following the suicide
attack.**

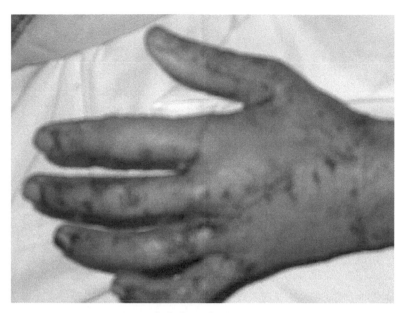

Brian's left hand after surgery.

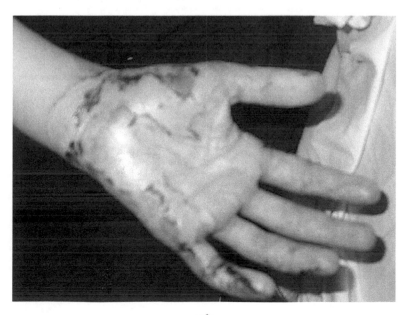

**Brian being awarded the Purple Heart
for wounds received in action.**

Brian's Purple Heart license plate: "NICETRY"

**Brian at the beginning of his career as an author and
speaker being introduced by his close friend and mentor,
Dave Roever, to an audience of over 10,000.**

**Brian and Jamie presenting a copy of their book and
movie to former President George W. Bush**

**Brian conducts Resiliency Training for thousands of troops
on military installations across the globe every year**

Brian led this small platoon of Marines who served together in the battle for Fallujah up to 11,400 ft. in the mountains of central Colorado as part of a resiliency expedition

Brian conducts several mentorship sessions and resiliency programs for troops and veterans each year

**Brian works closely with Unit Commanders
and coordinators to address key issues and solve
major problems facing their service members
and their families**

**Brian celebrating Veteran's Day by jumping
on the back of a 350-pound alligator
in the Florida Everglades**

**Brian and his wife Jamie in downtown
Fort Worth, Texas**

**Hanging out with Randy Couture at the
Gracie Barra MMA Gym in Westcliffe, CO**

ROBICHAUX

Chad in Afghanistan

Chad and Papa celebrating the Legacy FC Bantamwieght Title

3rd Force Recon Company during a HALO jump

**Chad's first Recon Plt. 1998 Del Bar Boat Basin-
Camp Pendleton,California**

**Chad doing Jiu-Jitsu training with the legendary
Master Carlos Gracie, Jr.**

**Chad with two of Jiu-Jitsu's all time best:
Prof. Draculino and Flavio Almeida**

**Chad kicking Humberto Deleon in the face on
Showtime's StrikeForce**

Big slam from Chad at Legacy FC

Chad in his first Black Belt Jiu-Jitsu Super Fight

(Photo courtesy of TXMMA.com)

Chad entering the cage at StrikeForce

**Chad swings a left hook over Bellator Champion Zach
Makovsky in the Main Event of Bellator on MTV2**

(Photo courtesy of TXMMA.com)

**Chad's victory over UFC Veteran Joseph Sandoval
after submitting him only 52 seconds into the first round.
(Photo courtesy of TXMMA.com)**

Chad wins the Legacy FC Bantamweight World Title

**Chad and friends after a grueling training session
at Randy Couture's house**

**Weigh-in at Strike Force, 131 lbs.
(Photo courtesy of MMAJunkie.com)**

**Train hard and win! Chad lands a kick
on friend and training partner Ricky Turcios**

**Walking to the cage for HD Net Fights
while former Recon Teammate and MARSOC
Operator Mark yells in my ear, "You are a meat eater!
Smash this vegetable eating #@$#@....."**

Chad and Kathy Robichaux

**Chad and Kathy Robichaux speaking and raising
awareness for the troops on Veteran's Day
at Resurrection Life Church in Michigan**

**Chad and Dave Roever speaking together
at the Fight Club Graduation**

Chad with his mentor, Steve Toth - TX Rep. State Legislature

Chad and Dave Roever with MG Anderson, Commanding General, 4th Infantry Division, Fort Carson, CO

Fight Club Graduation at Eagles Summit Ranch, CO

Never the Same
**Struggle and Success
After My Personal
Encounter with a
Suicide Bomber**

**Raw and graphic in
detail, Fleming
recalls his personal,
in-depth, first-hand
account about the
real story of the war
in Afghanistan and
how he overcame
the attack of a
suicide bomber
in Kandahar.**

**In The Red Chair
"Every Soul Has a
Story..." (DVD)**

**A suicide bomber
exploded 3-feet way
from him.**

He survived.

**Now, he tells his story
*IN THE RED CHAIR!***

Resources available at: www.BlownUpGuy.com

Everything the "MILITARY" Taught Me About Marriage

A Soldier's Perspective

by Brian Fleming

"The most unique book ever written on military marriages. A MUST READ!"

Fleming has written a groundbreaking book on the military's unique understanding of that most sacred of institutions: Marriage. Based on his years in the military and interaction with thousands of soldiers from all walks of life, he presents the most comprehensive illustration ever revealed concerning the military's understanding of matrimony. Brutally honest and humorously insightful, this work outlines everything the military knows about such topics as:

- **The Difference Between Vacation and Deployment**
- **Family Time**
- **How to Handle an Angry Military Spouse**
- **Neighborhood Sound Ordinance Levels**
- **Fidelity**
- **Common Sense**
  ...and more!

www.MilitaryMarriageAdvice.com

*To order REDEPLOYED in bulk or mass quantities for your organization, contact us today at:
info@briancfleming.com

OTHER MIGHTY OAKS RESOURCES

✪ An Unfair Advantage ✪
By Chad Robichaux

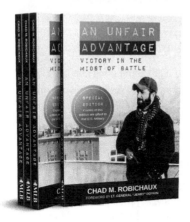

Take a journey with Force Recon Marine and Pro Mixed Martial Arts Champion Fighter, Chad Robichaux, as he shares a glimpse into the life of special operations, competition as a professional fighter, and the deep insight into this world's spiritual battles which we are all engaged. Chad shares personal stories of both success and failure experienced in Afghanistan, the MMA cage, and his biggest fight of all... coming home and facing a struggle with PTSD, a near divorce and almost becoming another veteran suicide statistic. Each chapter shares a parallel story of Biblical-time warriors who faced similar struggles and reveals *An Unfair Advantage* that led them to victory in the midst of those battles. Discover that same advantage for the battles you face and unlock the warrior spirit sewn in your heart by God Himself.

✪ Path to Resiliency ✪
By Chad Robichaux & Jeremy Stalnecker

This book was written to challenge the greatest of Warriors, whether military or civilian, man or woman... to be ready for, resilient to, and able to reintegrate from life's trials and rigors. You don't have to go to Iraq or Afghanistan to face the hardships and trials of life! Military service member or not, we all find ourselves in moments of adversity and hardship from time to time. When we do, will you have the resiliency to overcome.

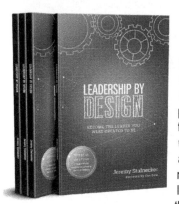

CPSIA information can be obtained
at www.ICGtesting.com
Printed in the USA
LVHW011216101119
636879LV00012B/903